The Field Is the World

The Field Is the World

A History of the Canton Mission
(1929–1949) of the Churches of Christ

by
Stephen V. Crowder

Foreword by
Thomas H. Olbricht

THE FIELD IS THE WORLD
A History of the Canton Mission (1929–1949) of the Churches of Christ

Copyright © 2018 Stephen V. Crowder. All rights reserved. Except for brief quotations in critical publications or reviews, no part of this book may be reproduced in any manner without prior written permission from the publisher. Write: Permissions, Wipf and Stock Publishers, 199 W. 8th Ave., Suite 3, Eugene, OR 97401.

Wipf & Stock
An Imprint of Wipf and Stock Publishers
199 W. 8th Ave., Suite 3
Eugene, OR 97401

www.wipfandstock.com

PAPERBACK ISBN: 978-1-5326-4366-8
HARDCOVER ISBN: 978-1-5326-4367-5
EBOOK ISBN: 978-1-5326-4368-2

Manufactured in the U.S.A.

Photos courtesy of Sidney D. Gamble Photographs, David M. Rubenstein Rare Book & Manuscript Library, Duke University

This work is dedicated to the memory

of the pioneer missionaries to China.

Contents

List of Figures | *viii*
Foreword | *xv*
   Thomas H. Olbricht
Acknowledgments | *xxiii*
Introduction | *xxv*

1. Years of Preparation (1921–1928) | 1
2. Establishment of the Canton Mission to the Onset of the Japanese Threat (1929–1937) | 14
3. Japanese Occupation and War Years (1938–1945) | 67
4. After the War to the Communist Takeover (1946–1949) | 75
5. Conclusion | 89

Appendix A | 95
   Operations of the Canton Mission
Appendix B | 101
   Religion and Doctrine
Appendix C | 108
   Hindrances to the Work
Appendix D | 115
   City of Canton in Photographs
Bibliography | 121
Index | 125

List of Figures

Figure 1.
Excerpt from *Word and Work*, December 1922 | 2

Figure 2.
The Bensons sailed for China on August 18, 1925, on the steamer Siberia | 3

Figure 3.
Hong Kong Mission Team, 1927 | 6

Figure 4.
Canton Bund | 10

Figure 5.
Canton meat market where the missionaries shopped | 11

Figure 6.
Canton street market for the purchasing of fresh fruit, vegetables, and dry goods | 12

Figure 7.
Front page of the *Oriental Christian* | 18

Figure 8.
Mr. Benson baptizes a Chinese convert in the Pearl River near Canton, 1930 | 19

Figure 9.
First Bible training class at the Canton Mission | 21

List of Figures

Figure 10.
Mr. T. W. So and his son, around 1933 | 22

Figure 11.
Mr. and Mrs. Ko and daughter, 1930 | 23

Figure 12.
Benson family in 1929, Canton, China | 25

Figure 13.
Page 28 of McGarvey's *Commentary on Acts*, depicting a scene from Acts chapter 2, with the heading "Biblical Pattern for Baptism." | 27

Figure 14.
Oldham family on furlough, 1933 | 29

Figure 15.
H. K. Leung and family in Canton, 1936 | 30

Figure 16.
Lowell Davis (left) and Roy Whitfield, shortly after their arrival in Canton in December of 1932 | 32

Figure 17.
First Class of the Canton Bible School, February 1933 | 33

Figure 18.
Congregants of the Kau Yuk Road Church of Christ | 35

Figure 19.
Typical street scene in Canton, with a barber and incense candlemaker working in the foreground and modest apartment housing in the background | 36

Figure 20.
Elizabeth Bernard and her mother, Mrs. Estella Bernard | 40

Figure 21.
House rented by the Bensons near the Bible school | 41

List of Figures

Figure 22.
Canton Bible School building during construction in September 1934 | 42

Figure 23.
Canton Bible School building before its formal opening in December 1934 | 43

Figure 24.
Mr. and Mrs. Davis shortly after the wedding ceremony | 44

Figure 25.
Spring Term of Canton Bible School, 1935 | 45

Figure 26.
English Preparatory School, fall of 1935 | 46

Figure 27.
A view inside the Bible school chapel. It was equipped with hardwood furniture, a concrete baptistry, and seating capacity for around 150 | 47

Figure 28.
Bible school kitchen, behind the main building | 47

Figure 29.
Dining hall and basketball court, behind school building | 48

Figure 30.
Small dining area inside the Bible school building | 48

Figure 31.
Girl's dormitory room, inside the Bensons' house | 48

Figure 32.
School for the Poor, Canton, China, 1935 | 51

Figure 33.
Neighborhood near the Canton Bible School, 1935 | 51

Figure 34.
Wedding photo of Ruth Gardner and Roy Whitfield | 52

LIST OF FIGURES

Figure 35.
The largest class of the Canton Bible School, Fall Term, 1936 | 57

Figure 36.
Kau Yuk Road Chapel in downtown Canton, November of 1936 | 58

Figure 37.
Missionary Team, Fall of 1936. Photo includes the Whitfields, Oldhams, Bernards, and Davises | 59

Figure 38.
The Whitfields on the porch of their rented house, spring, 1937 | 62

Figure 39.
Bible school commencement photo, June 1937 | 63

Figure 40.
Odessa Davis and daughter Avonelle in Macau, 1940 | 71

Figure 41.
Sampan Boat along the Pearl River in Canton | 72

Figure 42.
Davis family on furlough, 1945 | 73

Figure 43.
Mr. Davis with Mr. Leung (far left) and Mr. Wan (far right), Dean of the Southern Commercial College | 78

Figure 44.
Mr. Davis with students from the Southern Commercial College, in front of the Canton Bible School | 78

Figure 45.
Canton Mission Orphanage, 1948 | 80

Figure 46.
Frank and Earline Curtis with infant child, 1948 | 81

LIST OF FIGURES

Figure 47.
Senior Class of the Southern Commercial College, 1948 | 83

Figure 48.
Mr. Curtis tends the milking cows, 1948. | 84

Figure 49.
Frank and Earline Curtis at the orphanage, 1948. | 84

Figure 50.
Financial report for September 1936 (*OC*, October 1936). | 97

Figure 51.
Canton train depot (1930), memorial to Sun Yat-Sen (1935), flower pagoda of an Ancient Buddhist Temple (1935), and typical housing with a Catholic cathedral in the background (1930). | 116

Figure 52.
Island of Shameen viewed from bridge to Canton mainland, canal through poor neighborhood, ferry boat used to cross the Pearl River, and sampan boat, often used as living quarters for the poor. (These photos courtesy of Sidney D. Gamble Photographs, David M. Rubenstein Rare Book & Manuscript Library, Duke University.) | 117

Figure 53.
Canton YMCA, used by the missionary families for recreation and for occasionally holding English or religion classes (1920), Rickshaw puller (1935), Women laborers (1920), Woman laborer with young child (1920). (These photos courtesy of Sidney D. Gamble Photographs, David M. Rubenstein Rare Book & Manuscript Library, Duke University.) | 118

Figure 54.
Map of the southern provinces of Kwang Sai and Kwang Tung. Canton was the largest, most prominent city in the southern

List of Figures

region of China during the years of the Canton Mission. Its prominence in the region was one of the major factors in choosing Canton as the center for the missionary work. Map produced by Colleen Crowder Templeton. | 119

Foreword

STEPHEN CROWDER, IN *THE Field Is the World: A History of the Canton Mission (1929-1949) of the Churches of Christ*, provides a new and welcomed insight into Churches of Christ Missions. I will focus on the contribution Crowder makes to the history of Chinese missions, the role of Harding University administrators and professors in encouraging missions in China and elsewhere, and Stephen Crowder's legacy in respect to the key China missionaries.

Chinese Missions

Christian missionaries have been in China since the Roman Catholics in the fourteenth century and Protestants beginning in the nineteenth century. Crowder provides a brief history of these efforts. He reports on the numbers of professed Christians in China with about 800,000 Roman Catholics and 100,000 Protestants by 1900. Today some estimate the number of Christians in China as more than 60 million although various demographers dispute this number. Crowder's significant contribution lies in narrating a specific time frame—1929-1949—in regard to the efforts of Churches of Christ missionaries in China. His concrete details and photographs provide real-life depictions of those who went, their approaches, and their successes and failures. These are insights heretofore unavailable in a singular publication.

My wife and I have been interested in China from our youth because beginning in the 1930s we heard news reports regarding its occupation by Japan, China in World II, and the Communist takeover led by Mao Zedong. We have also been interested in Churches of Christ missions in China because we knew some of the missionaries involved. In 1984 we signed up for a People-to-People World Tour promoted by Dwight D. Eisenhower. We flew from San Francisco on Air China to Shanghai and spent nine days, then flew north to Beijing for seven days. Our group leaders were J. Jeffrey and Eleanor Auer of Indiana University and among those on the trip were two former speech professors of mine at Northern Illinois and the University of Iowa. The tour agenda was to visit historical sites, attend cultural events, and meet with communication peers in China. I would have relished contact with Christians, but such arrangements were not built into our schedule. On this trip I wondered about the work of George and Sallie Benson—the focal point for Crowder's book.

I normally wake up early. In Shanghai we stayed at a hotel located in the old German compound. A large park lay south of our hotel and all sorts of Chinese were doing slow, elegant Chinese exercises. I walked around the park and was surprised when I was stopped by three or four people who asked me in English if I was an American. When I responded yes, they proceeded to tell me that they had studied in the United States before World War II; one or two had taken courses at Yale Divinity School. I knew of the interest and involvement of Yale trained clerics in Chinese missions from the turn of the century. The importance of these early missions became increasingly vivid when set forth by Crowder in this work. One day I visited a commune of seventy-five thousand Chinese along with some of our group several miles out of Shanghai. As we traveled westward through the city, I had the eerie feeling that something was different. As I looked around it seemed as if I might be in an older European or American city. Though the buildings didn't look exactly the same because of bamboo structures and clothes lines. It finally dawned on me that what was different was that no church steeples were visible in any direction on the horizon. Crowder, in this book, sets out some of the historical reasons why Christian structures were scarce.

FOREWORD

Mission Instruction and Encouragement at Harding University

The early missionaries in Churches of Christ had special ties with Harding College (later University) of Searcy, Arkansas, founded there in 1924. The Harding University influence was especially true of the China Mission. For that reason, Crowder's book presents an important glimpse into the pre-World War II history of Churches of Christ missions. J. N. Armstrong (1870–1944) president of Harding 1924–1936 was influential in promoting missions. Armstrong taught several of the missionaries Crowder discusses in this book. The influence of Armstrong began at least as early as his presidency at Western Bible and Literary College in Odessa, Missouri, 1905–1907. I will focus on missionaries trained at Harding until about 1950. I knew several in my years at Harding (1947–49; 1954–55).

A number of missionaries who studied under Armstrong in Odessa went to Africa. The W. N. Shorts went in 1921 and J. Dow Merritt and wife in 1926. A. D. Brown, an MD, also went. Merritt was in Searcy on furlough when I was a student there in 1947–49, and Brown lived in Searcy and was a practicing physician. I also met the Shorts while at Harding.[1] William Brown, J. A. Britell, John and George Reese, and Myrtle Rowe also went to Africa. Those who went to Japan were O. D. Bixler and Omar Bixler, a nephew, son of Roy Bixler (Roy also attended Western), and E. A. Rhodes. There may also have been other missionaries who attended Western. Don Carlos Janes (1877–1944), born in Morgan County, Ohio, studied at Western. Janes lived in Louisville, Kentucky, at a later time. He was a one-man mission encourager and fund-raiser especially for missions in Japan and Cuba. He

---

1. The sources for the information in this foreword are: Gary Owen Turner, "Pioneer to Japan: A Biography of J. M. McCaleb," MA thesis, Abilene Christian, 1972. Charles R. Brewer, ed., *Missionary Pictorial* (Nashville: World Vision, 1966); *1979 Missionary Pictorial Supplement*, Lynn D. Yocum, ed. Don Carlos Janes, *Missionary Biographies* (Louisville: Janes, 1940–1943). Shawn Daggett, "The Lord Will Provide: James A. Harding and the Emergence of Faith Missions, 1892–1913," ThD diss., Boston University, 2007.

xvii

was associated with R. H. Boll (1875–1956) in Louisville. Most of these missionaries sent reports to *Word and Work*, edited by Boll. Janes supervised these reports. He took trips around the world to visit the missionaries, beginning in 1904. George S. Benson (1898–1991) who studied under Armstrong at Harper College in Kansas helped plant congregations in China from 1925 to 1936. Sallie Benson knew the Armstrongs when she studied at Cordell Christian College in Cordell, Oklahoma. Armstrong served as president of Cordell from 1908–1918. L. C. Sears, the son-in-law of the Armstrongs, became a teacher at Cordell and later a dean at Harper College. The legacy of James A. Harding (after whom Harding University was named), his daughter Woodson Harding Armstrong, and their daughter Pattie Hathaway Armstrong Sears and son-in-law L. C. Sears is told in their granddaughter's book: *The Greatest Work in the World: Education as a Mission of Early Twentieth-Century Churches of Christ: Letters of Lloyd Cline Sears and Pattie Hathaway Armstrong*, edited by Elizabeth Cline Parsons (Eugene: Wipf and Stock, 2015).

Other persons who attended Harding and became missionaries before 1945 were: Stanton Garrett, who went to Rhodesia in 1930; Alvin Hobby, Zambia and Rhodesia, 1938; and J. C. Shewmaker, Zambia, 1939. A new surge of Churches of Christ missions occurred after World War II. The leadership of the churches increasingly took up the challenge of taking the gospel into all the world. Many members of the churches traveled abroad during the war either in the military or in organizations connected with war operations. Their travels opened their eyes. Various leaders encouraged mission undertakings, chief among whom was Otis Gatewood (1911–1999), who spoke on campus at least twice when I was a student at Harding and also in the fifties when I taught there.

When I arrived at Harding in the fall of 1947 I ran into many people excited about missions. I'm not sure it was all prompted by Harding teachers. Andy T. Ritchie Jr. encouraged evangelism of all sorts, but especially in areas in the United States where Churches of Christ were few. George Benson (president of Harding 1936–1965) certainly encouraged foreign missions, but that was one among many agendas he pursued. He spent far more of his time raising funds for Harding and getting his National Education Program off the ground. Harding College had no one on the faculty assigned to teach mission courses in the late forties. It seems to me that J. Dow Merritt, who was on furlough, may have taught a course in missions and had a group meeting in his residence to encourage missions. Other families lived in Searcy who had been involved in missions, among them the Lawyer family, who had worked in Africa. Various mission study groups sprang up on campus focusing on specific countries, for example, Japan and Germany. I attended the German group even though I did not plan to be a German missionary. My sister, Nedra Jo Olbricht McGill, however, hoped to spend time in Germany. She graduated from Harding in 1949 and after marrying James R. McGill in 1955, they spent 1960–62 in Nürnberg and München, Germany. Missionaries—for example, Keith Coleman, who was in Germany, and Dieter Alten, who was studying at Lipscomb but who went back to Germany to preach, and Joe Cannon, who went to Japan—spoke at the Harding chapel and elsewhere.

In the late 1940s several former Harding students departed from the United States. J. C. Reid went to Zambia in 1947; Robert Helsten, 1948 to Germany, later to Switzerland; Jack Nadeau to Germany; Samuel Timmerman in 1948 to Belgium, and Joe Cannon, 1947; Robert Harry Fox Jr., 1949, and George Gurganus to Japan. Most of these people knew each other while on the Harding campus.

Several who went to Germany were classmates of mine (except Glenn Olbricht, 1959 to Nürnberg, my brother). He would have been a classmate had I stayed at Harding long enough to graduate. Bob Hare first worked in Germany in 1950 then Austria, Ted Nadeau (brother of Jack Nadeau) went to Germany 1950, and Glenn Boyd, 1958, ended up in Heidelberg. Bob and Barbara Morris went to Karlsruhe in 1958. Bob was a talented opera singer and sang in German opera companies. L. T. Gurganus went to Japan. He was the nephew of George P. Gurganus. His support was typical in that several Alabama churches contributed to his funds. L. T. was born in Gordova, Alabama, and his father L. T. Sr. still lived there. Others were Carmelo Casella, 1958, and Rodney Wald, 1955–59 (my Harding roommate) to Australia. Jerry Porter went to Scotland in 1959, Jack Meredith, 1958 to Puerto Rico, Bert Perry 1950 (a Canadian and older student when I was at Harding) to the Philippines, and Charles W. Davis 1955 to the Philippines, Kenneth Rideout 1950 went to Thailand. Ken was related to Dortha Rideout Taylor, my Uncle Tom Taylor's wife. J. L. and Margaret Crumpet Roberts commenced mission work in Belgium in 1954. Margaret was my chemistry lab instructor in several courses. Truman Scott went to Italy sometime in the 1950s.

Indeed, Harding College was a training ground for missionaries and their families. Stephen Crowder has therefore given us a window from which we can look into the background of those who undertook missions to foreign lands in Churches of Christ. The Bensons, the Oldhams, the Davises, the Whitfields, the Broadduses, and others mentioned by Crowder in this book are very important links in the history of missions in Churches of Christ.

The Stephen Crowder Legacy

Crowder became interested in the Canton Mission because the key leaders, George and Sallie Benson, were his grandparents. His mother, Ruth Benson Crowder, in her early years grew up at the mission. I first met Stephen's parents in Iowa soon after they were married. His father, Numa Crowder, was the minister for a congregation in Muscatine. The Crowders later moved to Macomb, Illinois. We lived in Iowa City, where I preached and took graduate courses at the University of Iowa. The Crowders and the Olbrichts shared an occasional meal. I first met Stephen at Abilene Christian University. He attended the Minter Lane Church of Christ, where I was an elder. I was chair of the Religion Division at Pepperdine University, Malibu, California, 1986–1996. After retiring I continued to offer graduate courses in biblical theology in the

FOREWORD

Pepperdine off-campus programs. Stephen enrolled in the course I offered in our Albuquerque programs in the early 2000s.

The Bensons were important in Churches of Christ and also in national history. Books by Edward Hicks and John C. Stevens have been published about the Bensons, but neither Hicks nor Stevens spent much time on the Chinese mission's aspect of the Benson story.[2] They focus more on the return of the Bensons to the United States and George S. Benson's presidency of Harding University. Stephen undertook major research in original, published, and unpublished sources in order to write this book. He possesses or has available numerous family documents, photos, and diaries. He has also visited other pertinent archives and utilized periodicals, not all of which are readily available. He has incorporated several important pictures and maps into the text. Crowder has opened up an exceptional window into Churches of Christ missions in China.

Thomas H. Olbricht
Distinguished Professor Emeritus of Religion
Pepperdine University

---

2. L. Edward Hicks, *Sometimes in the Wrong, but Never in Doubt: George Benson and the Education of the New Religious Right* (Knoxville: University of Tennessee Press, 1994); John C. Stevens, *Before Any Were Willing: The Story of George S. Benson* (Searcy, AR: Harding University Press, 1991).

Acknowledgments

THE AUTHOR WOULD LIKE to thank Avonelle Davis and Gladys Whitfield Pedigo for graciously sharing many important letters and photos from the archives of the Davis and Whitfield families. Hannah Wood, Harding University archivist, made available many valuable journal articles, photos, and letters relevant to this work. Her support is greatly appreciated. Thanks to David Lee for translating the Chinese characters on numerous photos, and for sharing personal insights on life and religion in China. Thanks also to Mike Tune for sharing photos and the biography of Elizabeth Bernard, and to Victor Leung for sharing photos of the Leung family. And finally, a special thank you to Professor Thomas Olbricht for writing an insightful foreword and for encouraging me to complete this work.

Introduction

PROTESTANT MISSIONARIES BEGAN ARRIVING in China in the early 1800s, first with limited success, then followed by expansion from 1860 to 1900. The Roman Catholic Church had arrived in China much earlier, with limited success for centuries, but as of 1860 had recovered lost gains and counted converts between 250,000 and 300,000. This number grew to between 700,000 and 800,000 by 1900, while Protestant numbers had grown to 100,000 by 1900.[1]

As these numbers continued to increase, the period from roughly 1920 to 1930 became the high point for foreign missionary work in China. In 1925, about 3,000 missionaries from the Roman Catholic Church were laboring in China, while the Protestant count, including the wives of missionaries, totaled about 8,000. The number of Protestant converts had risen to about 400,000 while the number of Catholic converts was estimated to be about 2,200,000.[2]

A small but significant part of this explosion in missionary work included missionaries from the Stone-Campbell tradition. The movement's missionary presence in China began in the mid-1880s, when the Disciples of Christ sent physician William Macklin to establish a mission in Nanking.[3] Other missionaries soon followed, and by 1925 this work had established fourteen congregations with a total membership of 1,400. Several day

---

1. Bays, *New History*, 77.
2. Latourette, *History of Christian Missions in China*, 3.
3. Williams et al., *Stone-Campbell Movement*, 117.

INTRODUCTION

schools had been established, as well as work at several universities and Christian hospitals. At its high point in 1926, the Disciples of Christ supported sixty-four missionaries in China.[4]

The North American Churches of Christ first sent missionaries to China in the mid-1920s, when George and Sallie Benson were sent to southern China in 1925. Others soon followed, with the group first working in Hong Kong before moving to the port city of Canton (Guangzhou) to establish a mission there. In the mid-1920s Canton displayed evidence of decades of Christian missionary work, including the extensive campus of Lingnan University, the True Light Seminary for girls, and buildings of a Protestant Union Theological Seminary. A large Protestant hospital had been constructed along the bund, as well as many church buildings and the Young Men's Christian Association. The presence of a Roman Catholic Church was also visible in the twin towers of its impressive cathedral.[5] The Canton Mission of the Churches of Christ labored there from its beginning in 1929 until its forced closing in 1949 due to the Communist takeover and expulsion of all foreign missionaries.

The purpose of this book is to provide a detailed account of the tireless, dedicated work of this small group of missionaries. The account will include the difficult years of preparation (1921–1928), the establishment of the Canton Mission to the onset of the Japanese threat (1929–1937), the heroic efforts during the Japanese occupation and war years (1938–1945), and finally, its work after the war until the Communist takeover (1946–1949).

Emphasis will be on the people and their work, including both the American missionaries and their dedicated Chinese coworkers. Their philosophies and strategies for missionary work, clearly shaped by their Stone-Campbell heritage, will be highlighted. The pioneering work, with its successes, failures, and lessons learned, will be discussed. Finally, an attempt will be made to assess the significance of the Canton Mission of the Churches of Christ within the historical framework of the Stone-Campbell movement.

4. Ibid., 255.
5. Latourette, *History of Christian Missions in China*, 4.

Introduction

In researching the life of my grandmother, Sallie Hockaday Benson (1896–1981), I discovered a wealth of material on her years spent in China as a missionary from 1925–1936. It was apparent that she and her coworkers in the Canton Mission had a very compelling and important story. This project is a result of researching that story. I have relied mainly on material produced by the missionaries themselves. The articles they wrote that appeared in the *Canton Christian* and the *Oriental Christian* were invaluable. The books, letters, diaries, and photos from the family archives of the Bensons, Oldhams, Davises, and Whitfields also added immensely to the work. Valuable secondary sources included the epic work *A History of Christian Missions in China*, by Latourette, and the *New History of Christianity in China*, by Bays. Churches of Christ publications during the era of the Canton Mission, including *Word and Work*, *Gospel Advocate*, and *Firm Foundation*, provided valuable insight as well.

1

Years of Preparation (1921–1928)

Bensons and Oldhams

GEORGE S. BENSON (1898–1991) was raised in western Oklahoma, and in 1921 enrolled in Harper College, a junior college in Harper, Kansas, operated by the Churches of Christ. Its president was J. N. Armstrong, a restoration preacher and educator in the Stone-Campbell tradition who would have great influence on Benson and many of the future missionaries of the Canton Mission. While Armstrong rarely preached to persuade anyone to become a foreign missionary, he preached to "develop a real spirit of Christian service in the hearts of his students."[1]

At Harper College, Mr. Benson met Lewis T. Oldham (1903–1985), who shared his desire to do mission work abroad. The two formed a study group and explored various possibilities for mission work. They were greatly influenced by the Churches of Christ publications that promoted mission work. Articles such as the one below, proclaiming the Chinese "ready for the gospel,"[2] inspired

---

1. George Benson, "Plan with a Purpose," 4. Many years later, Benson considered Armstrong to have been the most influential person in his life.

2. Janes, "On Foreign Fields," 375. Don Carlos Janes, writing in the Churches of Christ publication *Word and Work*, frequently attempted to generate interest in foreign missions. He later became a forwarding agent for the Canton Mission.

> December, 1922   375
> Word and Work
>
> # ON FOREIGN FIELDS
> ## *MISSIONARY NOTES*
> Don Carlos Janes
>
> Who carries the gospel to China? ** The scriptures are inspired; Jesus Christ is the supernaturally begotten son of God; the Golden Rule is still binding; and we need to send some one among the Chinese, many of whom are ready for the gospel.

Excerpt from *Word and Work*, December 1922

them to consider China as a possibility for mission work. They soon discovered that China was the largest country in population in the world, yet had no missionaries from the Churches of Christ. From that point forward, they were both committed to missionary work in China. They agreed that after they finished college, they would begin a mission work there.

After completing their studies at Harper and then Oklahoma A&M, both Mr. Benson and Mr. Oldham moved to Harding College in Morrilton, Arkansas, where Armstrong had become the new college's first president. Benson finished school at Harding during the 1924-1925 school year while also working as principal of the Harding Academy. With the encouragement and limited financial support from the Morrilton Church of Christ, plans for China were finalized. The Bensons would leave for China in 1925 and the Oldhams would follow after Mr. Oldham's graduation in 1927.

By this time both men had married, Mr. Benson to Sallie E. Hockaday (1896-1981) and Mr. Oldham to Grace E. Narron (1904-1982). Sallie had attended Cordell Christian College in Cordell, Oklahoma, where Armstrong had been president prior to his move to Harper College. While at Cordell, Sallie had the opportunity to hear many great restoration preachers, including James A. Harding, the father-in-law of Armstrong. Inspired by the preaching she heard, as well as the influence of Armstrong, Sallie became interested in foreign mission work, and determined that given the opportunity, she would do mission work abroad. After teaching at various high schools in Texas and Oklahoma, Sallie was hired by Armstrong to teach at the Harding Academy. It was there that she met and married George Benson. Just six weeks after their wedding in July of 1925, the Bensons left for China.

The Bensons sailed for China on August 18, 1925, on the steamer Siberia

Grace Narron had met her future husband at Harper College, and likewise shared his desire for foreign mission work. They married in August of 1924, completed college together at Harding in June of 1927, and left for China in September of 1927. Both Sallie Hockaday Benson and Grace Narron Oldham were equal partners with their husbands and would work tirelessly in the mission field of China. The Bensons and Oldhams would together establish the Canton Mission and would be dedicated leaders and coworkers at the mission for most of a decade.

Into the Interior of China

Two months after arriving in Hong Kong in September of 1925, the Bensons embarked upon a trip into the interior of Kwang Sai (Guangxi) Province to work with an older missionary couple at an orphanage in the village of Kwei Hsien. The six months that followed in the interior were extremely difficult, due to both a strong anti-foreign spirit and the Bensons lack of preparation. The perilous trip up the West River 350 miles beyond the coastal city of Canton took an entire week on the steamship Chung On, with robbers and pirates a constant threat. Five months after marrying and leaving Sallie's hometown of Granite, Oklahoma, the Bensons arrived at Kwei Hsien.

The Bensons worked and lived at the Faith and Love Mission, an orphanage providing care for sixty-five mostly blind children. Sallie wrote that learning the language was the "first big mountain to climb"[3] and that the written language was even more difficult than the spoken language. Daily language lessons started in earnest, but progress was very slow.

After five relatively peaceful months in Kwei Hsien, problems arose in April of 1926. With anti-foreign sentiment at a fever pitch, a mob of students and soldiers, spurred on by Russian Bolshevik sympathizers, threatened the mission, chanting, "Kill the foreign devils."[4] Friendly local officials recommended to the Bensons that they leave the village for their own safety. With Sallie's health also an issue, the Bensons returned down the West River to the coast and the safety of Hong Kong. Due to the anti-foreign outbreak of 1925, missionary accomplishments throughout China had been "shaken from center to circumference."[5] By 1925, 102 different missionary societies and 6,000 missionaries were listed as present

---

3. Sallie Benson, *Chats about China*, 43. The Bensons' first year in China was an extremely difficult one, living in the interior of Kwang Sai Province, where few English speakers were found, and foreign hostilities were the greatest. Sallie was expecting their first child, Ruth, when the Bensons made the decision to return to the coast.

4. Ibid, 101.

5. Ibid, 124.

in China, but few remained in the interior, with most living and working along the coast. Because of the persistent political turmoil and threat of violence, the Bensons would never return deep into the interior. However, the time spent in Kwei Hsien provided valuable lessons regarding the language, culture, and anti-foreign sentiment. These lessons would prove to be of great value to the Bensons in their future work in the Canton Mission.

Hong Kong Mission

Later that year, the Bensons welcomed a baby girl, Ruth, on November 30, 1926, born at Matilda hospital in Hong Kong. At Sham Shui Po, they found a small congregation of "earnest believers," working independently of any foreign influence. One member had been a member of the Christian Church in the United States, and the preacher had worked three years in Australia with a Church of Christ. Benson reported that they led the church to a "better knowledge of the word," convincing them to give up its use of instrumental music and to discontinue having a woman preacher occasionally.[6] Mr. Benson held a short meeting, preaching with the aid of an interpreter, and a handful were baptized. He also taught an English Bible class for the young Chinese that knew some English. The Bensons were confident that when they left, the congregation could continue its work without the further help of a missionary.

In October of 1927, the Bensons were joined as planned in Hong Kong by the Oldhams, also now with a baby daughter, Frances. Other missionaries joining the Hong Kong work in 1927 were Emmett and Margaret Broaddus. Miss Ethel Mattley had joined the Bensons in Hong Kong late in 1926. The Sham Shui Po Church of Christ became the base of mission work for the group

---

6. George Benson, letter to supporters from Hong Kong, December 24, 1926. The use of instrumental music was a major controversy early in the history of the Stone-Campbell movement. The Churches of Christ opposition to its use was one of the major factors in it becoming a separate religious communion, officially recognized in 1906. See Foster et al., *Encyclopedia of the Stone-Campbell Movement*, 414–17, for a discussion of this controversy.

that would remain in Hong Kong when the Bensons and Oldhams moved to establish the Canton Mission. The Broaddus family and Miss Mattley would be frequent visitors at the Canton Mission from their station in Hong Kong, and would also establish smaller missions in the interior of Kwang Sai Province. The photo below shows the Benson family with infant Ruth, Miss Mattley, and Chinese coworkers in Hong Kong in 1927.

Hong Kong Mission Team, 1927

Their final year in Hong Kong was 1928, an important year of preparation for both the Oldhams and Bensons. Mr. Oldham oversaw a new work in the Hung Hom section of Hong Kong. He prepared the young church to assume the total responsibility of the work there as soon as was reasonably possible. The Oldhams studied the language four hours a day with a Chinese teacher and spent another four hours preparing their lessons. Mr. Oldham was a quick study in the written language, learning five new characters per day. This was invaluable preparation for the translation and publication work that he would lead as part of the Canton Mission team.

In April of 1928 the missionaries in Hong Kong were visited by George Pepperdine, then president of the Western Auto Supply Company. He encouraged and gave financial assistance to the Bensons to hold a three-month campaign in the Philippines. The Bensons went to the Philippine Islands for the summer months and had success there. During the work in Mindoro seventy-nine Filipinos were baptized and at Pinamalayan another fifty-five were baptized. Although tempted by this success to stay in the Philippines, the Bensons hearts were "tied to China,"[7] and the decision was made to return to China.

The women contributed greatly to the mission work in Hong Kong. Ethel Mattley and Sallie Benson were the leaders of the work among the Chinese women. The cultural constraints of China made their work invaluable. The Chinese men desiring baptism often wanted to wait until the women of their families could be taught and baptized, as well. However, custom precluded the male missionaries from teaching the Chinese women, so women missionaries were desperately needed to teach them. With the help of a Christian Chinese woman, Mrs. Lo, house-to-house visitation and teaching was accomplished by both Miss Mattley and Mrs. Benson.

That same year Mr. Benson and Mr. Oldham traveled around Kwang Tung (Guangdong) Province, looking for a promising location to begin a new mission work on the mainland. They discovered that nearly every city of any size in the province already had one or more mission stations,[8] although the fields visited were not viewed as adequately worked. This observation would later inform the decision to locate in the city of Canton.

---

7. Benson, George, letter to supporters from Hong Kong, November 20, 1928.

8. Ibid.

The mission team was faced with the decision to go into one of the "neglected" corners of South China, or go to one of the urban centers where other church missions were already well established. The Bensons and Oldhams believed that their proposed work was "for the restoration of the New Testament church," and to restore the "New Testament pattern".[9] The existing missions were not viewed as adequate to fulfill this purpose. This belief, and the developing mission strategy, led them to favor a major urban center. The choice for the new mission work would be Canton.

In reflecting on their first three years in China, Mr. Benson's assessment of the work was mixed:

> We wish we could report that during these three years we had seen thousands of Chinese people come to know and to trust in Jesus Christ, the Savior of the world. But instead we must report that only a few have been led to know and to worship the true God. However, with each additional year in China, as we get more of the language, we are able to feel more satisfaction from our work. The last year has been the best one.[10]

By November of 1928, the anti-foreign and anti-missionary sentiment had subsided in South China, and the political conditions had also improved somewhat. The churches in Hong Kong were largely self-sustaining with little additional assistance needed from foreign missionaries, so the time was right for a move to the mainland of China. In February of 1929, the decision was announced that the Bensons and Oldhams would move their mission work to Canton.[11]

A Brief History of Canton (Guangzhou)

Canton, known as the "cradle of revolution,"[12] was the seat of the revolutionary movement under Sun Yat-Sen. He triggered the

9. Ibid.
10. Ibid.
11. George Benson, letter to supporters from Canton, February 22, 1929.
12. Tsin, *Nation, Governance and Modernity in China*, 9.

Years of Preparation (1921–1928)

protests that eventually resulted in the collapse of the Qing Dynasty (1644–1911) and the formation of the Republic of China in 1911. Sun was appointed provisional president of the republic and later cofounded and led the Nationalist Party of China. In 1918, the city's first urban council was established and "Guangzhou" became the official name of the city.

From Canton, the Nationalist armies of Chiang Kai-shek marched northward in the 1920s to establish a central government in Nanjing. During the early 1920s, Canton retained its rebellious streak. The city saw a number of protests led by students and workers against the continued foreign presence. Some of these demonstrations were met with bloody violence from foreign troops, and more strikes were called in retaliation. Canton even acquired the nickname "Red City"[13] among some observers, an uncanny omen since one of the first communes in China was established there, albeit briefly, under Soviet guidance in 1927.

Canton was also known as a progressive city. Most of the Chinese who had traveled and studied abroad were from Canton, and the people of Canton were more likely to be receptive to foreigners.[14] It was the capital of Kwang Tung Province, and was the political, social, and educational center of South China.

At the onset of US involvement in World War II, Canton was an occupied city. The Japanese bombed the city persistently beginning in the fall of 1937, entered Canton in October of 1938, and stayed until the end of the war in 1945.[15] Following the war, Communist forces defeated the Nationalist armies and entered the city on October 14, 1949, signaling the Communist takeover of China. All foreign missionaries were expelled from China. The Communist government attempted some renewal projects to improve the lives of its Canton residents, including new housing along the Pearl River for the poor boat people. Canton was further developed as an industrial center and a modern port, trading with Hong

---

13. Spence, *Search for Modern China*, 343.
14. Ho, *Understanding Canton*, 4.
15. Perkins, "Guangdong Province," 193.

Kong, and reclaimed its place as one of Chinas most prosperous and thriving cities.

Living in Canton During the 1930s

During the 1930s, Canton was a vibrant city in transition. Major infrastructure improvement programs were carried out from the turn of the century into the 1930s, during which modern, wide streets were built to replace many of its narrow streets and winding alleys. Waterworks projects were completed, modern sewers introduced, an electrical lighting plant was built, modern Western-style department stores were established, and many new parks were created.[16] The "bund," the embankment along the Pearl river, was extended, allowing the city to expand to the south to its present waterfront. The photo below shows the bustling bund area of Canton in 1930.

Canton Bund

Automobiles mingled with rickshaws, and modern department stores attracted both the wealthy and the poor, who often

16. Tsin, *Nation, Governance and Modernity in China*, 57–58.

lived their entire lives in boats along the bund. Modern factories were surrounded by small shops with local merchants peddling their produce and wares on the street.

Canton meat market where the missionaries shopped

**Canton street market for the purchasing of fresh fruit,
vegetables, and dry goods**

Canton was one of the five Chinese treaty ports opened by the Treaty of Nanking, signed in 1842, at the end of the First Opium War between the United Kingdom and China. The other ports were Fuzhou, Xiamen, Ningbo, and Shanghai. Canton remained one of the most important ports through the end of the Qing dynasty.

With the end of the Qing dynasty, outside investors were eager to invest in the new Canton. One of the first significant investments was the modern department store. In 1912, the Sincere Company opened its first store in China on the midwestern section of the Canton Bund. The five-story Sincere building featured an impressive stock of merchandise as well as an amusement park on the top floor featuring live performances and movies. It was a favorite attraction for tourists and residents of Canton. The Daxin Department store was a modern seven-story building located further west on the Bund that featured its own rooftop entertainment center. With the construction of new department stores, cinemas, and other entertainment centers, the bund became an attraction for the "rich, the curious, and the unsavory."[17] Every imaginable modern product was available to the Canton missionaries at some price, but limited budgets encouraged thriftiness, and clothing as well as other donations from home were always greatly appreciated.

Canton's climate posed various challenges for the missionaries. Its subtropical monsoon climate, typical of southeastern China, included a spring season with typically muggy weather, and a long, wet, hot, and humid summer season.[18] During the summers, the missionaries would seek relief from the heat by taking trips to the local mountains. The winter months were typically dry and mild without snow, with temperatures rarely falling below 40° F. As a result, none of the buildings in Canton were heated, and shipments of warm clothing from home were always welcome. The average annual rainfall of about sixty-four inches brought a year-round growing season. Fresh produce was usually available in the street markets, but the missionaries could not eat it due to unsanitary growing practices used by local farmers. It was important for new arrivals to Canton to quickly learn safe dietary practices, as amoebic dysentery was a constant threat.

17. Ibid, 59.
18. Perkins, "Chinese Climate," 95.

2

Establishment of the Canton Mission to the Onset of the Japanese Threat (1929–1937)

Deciding on Canton

IN THE *ORIENTAL CHRISTIAN* of January 1931, Mr. Benson reflected on the mission team's decision to locate in a major center of China. Their initial thinking was to select a location where no other missionaries were already working. They soon discovered that there were already more than a hundred different missionary societies working in China and that virtually every section of the country had been "claimed" by one or more missionary groups. In particular, there was no corner in South China that was not being worked by at least one missionary society. Only extremely remote, mountainous, and sparsely populated regions had no previous missionary work. They believed that to work in such a region would greatly hinder future progress in China, as their goal was to start a work that would take their message to all of China. They also believed that their message and goals were unique. Benson commented:

> We wish to see New Testament practices observed, and congregations built up after the New Testament pattern throughout China. Should we work only in the more

remote districts, leaving the centers and strategic locations to others, our purpose would be largely defeated from the outset.¹

Mr. Benson later wrote that "if our message were no different than that of the denominations, I would be ready to leave China tomorrow."²

The mission team had also discovered while in Hong Kong that their work would be greatly dependent on Chinese helpers, and such helpers would be more readily available in a major center. This thinking, and other realities of missionary work, led the team to decide upon a major center for their new mission work. The work established and grounded in a major center, they believed, would in the long run also be best for the work in the interior. It would provide a foothold from which work could be advanced into the more remote regions of the province. This strategy represented a major change in philosophy from when the mission team first went to China.

The Bensons and Oldhams believed that Canton was the logical place to establish the new mission center. Their training to date in the Cantonese language limited the work to the two southern provinces of China, Kwang Sai and Kwang Tung, and in these two provinces Canton was clearly the "hub of the wheel." From this center, once churches were well established, the work could then expand outward into the villages and hamlets of these provinces. Other mission teams would need to be recruited and trained to establish work in the major centers of China's other provinces.

The physical safety of the missionary families, now both with young children, was also a major concern. Anti-foreign and anti-missionary sentiment was a threat that could resurface at any time with little warning. The American consul at Canton had strongly advised the missionaries not to go into the distant interior, but to locate only at easily accessible points. Missionaries who insisted on going farther into the interior would be allowed to, but they could

1. George Benson, "Realities," January 1931, 5.
2. George Benson, "Present Activities," 4.

not expect assistance if trouble came.[3] The decision to establish the mission center in Canton would prove to be a wise one when the Japanese threat came in 1937.

Move to Open the Canton Mission (February 1929)

The move to Canton, and the strategies that would be used there, were announced in a letter to supporters in the United States in February of 1929. The mission team had learned early on that the Chinese people were not eagerly waiting, "ready for the gospel," as advertised by an optimistic church publication. A definite program with a definite goal was needed to deliver their message to the Chinese people. Benson and Oldham were greatly influenced by the writings of Latourette on the history of mission work in China.[4] This history included a summary of both Catholic and Protestant missionary methods, how they differed, and what had been most successful. Latourette emphasized schooling and other educational efforts that had been made by previous Protestant missionaries to China. Mr. Benson and Mr. Oldham concluded that a Bible training school would be an imperative, to teach and train men and women to serve as teachers, evangelists, elders, and church workers. Mr. Benson desired to lead this part of the Canton Mission work by conducting a small Bible training school to prepare workers to eventually take the message throughout the southern provinces.

A second part of successful work would be to produce high-quality Christian literature in Chinese, as the value of the printed page was especially great in China. While the spoken language of the south, Cantonese, was different than that of the north, Mandarin, the written language was very similar in both north and south. Literature prepared in the south could thus be used in the north where other missionaries were working. Previous missionaries

---

3. George Benson, letter to supporters from Hong Kong, November 20, 1928.

4. Latourette, *History of Christian Missions in China*.

who had been most successful were those who had sent native Chinese workers ahead of them with an abundance of literature. Therefore, to "restore the New Testament order in the Church,"[5] good literature was needed. While much of China was illiterate, the educated people in the population centers always desired more to read.

Mr. Oldham was especially talented in languages, and had made great progress in both spoken and written Chinese, so he was ideally suited to lead the literature work. He had been fortunate to secure the assistance of a well-educated Chinese man, So Tin Wong, who read and spoke both English and Chinese. Together they would publish tracts, booklets, and books in Chinese. Both the literature work and the Bible training work would prove to be valuable assistance to the work that the Broaddus family and Ethel Mattley would later do in the interior of Kwang Sai Province.

The literature work and the Bible training work were the necessary means to the accomplishment of the one main end, active evangelistic work. The Canton Mission would first establish churches within the city of Canton, then start new work in smaller villages throughout the province. As soon as a newly established church could become self-sustaining, the missionary would then move to a new village. The literature work, the Bible training work, and the active evangelistic work would be the threefold strategy adopted and used by the Canton Mission from its establishment in early 1929 until its forced closure at the hands of the Communists in 1949.

Getting to Work in Canton

The mission team established living quarters in Canton in an apartment building off of the narrow street called "Man Sing Sun Kaai," with the Bensons living on the second floor and the Oldhams on the third.

---

5. George Benson, letter to supporters from Canton, February 22, 1929.

The literature work was soon turning out many tracts and booklets. By April of 1930, over 30,000 pieces of literature had been published, including 5,000 copies of a booklet, "The Infallibly Safe Way."[6] The mission team also started publishing the *Canton Christian*, a twelve-page quarterly whose purpose was to "acquaint the readers with the activities and progress of the missionaries on the field; to acquaint them with the Chinese people, and to stimulate missionary interest."[7] This publication was the first of its kind in the Churches of Christ, having been published in the mission field and sent to churches and various supporters in America. It remained a quarterly through January of 1931. In April of 1931, its name was changed to *Oriental Christian*, and it was published as an eight-page monthly from that time through its last edition in September of 1937. As the *Oriental Christian*, it broadened its scope beyond the Canton work, and regularly included updates from the Philippines, Japan, and other China work. Each of the missionaries contributed articles updating the progress in their particular mission field or area of emphasis. Mrs. Oldham and Mrs. Benson at various times contributed the column "Children's Page," informing the younger readers in America of the day-to-day activities of their families in China.

Front page of the *Oriental Christian*

The phrase "The Field Is the World," used for the title of this project, was often printed on the front page of the *Oriental Christian*. It served as a reminder to both readers and to the missionaries themselves of the biblical directive to Christians to take their message to all nations.

6. Lewis Oldham, "Financial Report," 15. This booklet outlined a "plan of salvation" consistent with the mainstream doctrine of the Churches of Christ from its early history.

7. George Benson, "Canton Christian," 3.

Later in 1929, Mr. Benson began "making tents," teaching English three hours a day at the newly founded Sun Yat-Sen University in Canton to earn extra income to help support the evangelistic work. The hours spent in preparation, teaching, private tutoring, and grading consumed much of his time, however, and the evangelistic work suffered, with very little initial progress. With the money received from teaching, however, a building was rented for evangelistic work in the west part of the city, on Tung Shan Fong Road. The building was painted and furnished with good seating. A Chinese evangelist and his wife, Mr. and Mrs. Ko, were hired for full-time work there. The chapel was opened in January of 1930, with an original membership of eight. From the opening, there was evangelistic preaching six nights each week, with an average attendance of a hundred on weeknights and more than a hundred on Sunday. The membership quickly increased from eight to seventeen. The mission team believed that this

Mr. Benson baptizes a Chinese convert in the Pearl River near Canton, 1930

"street preaching" approach was the most effective way of getting the work started in Canton.[8] Plans were made to use one of the rooms in the chapel for a special six-week Bible study course to begin in January of 1930. The evangelistic work also included support for the work in Mui Luk, a city within Kwang Tung Province where a small church had been started in 1927.

Mrs. Benson taught a small class of children every Sunday, and taught a kindergarten class for Chinese children five days each week. She also took on a small English class to earn a little extra income, teaching two nights a week for the nurses and workers at the nearby hospital. She tried to encourage the students to attend the Sunday worship services, and would often "sprinkle a little gospel salt" into her English lessons.[9]

In surveying the local missionary landscape at the close of 1929, Benson lamented the fact that their "undenominational preaching" of the gospel was "eighty years behind" the Baptist missionary work in Canton. He used this as an appeal to supporters in America "to pray, to come, and to give" for the advancement of the work in China.[10]

First Bible Training Class

The first Bible training class at the Canton Mission, pictured below, was conducted over a six-week period in January and February of 1930.

---

8. George Benson, "Two Steps by Faith," 7.
9. Sallie Benson, "Personal Glimpses," 7.
10. George Benson, "Eighty Years Behind," 14.

Establishment of the Canton Mission

First Bible training class at the Canton Mission

The teachers were Mr. Benson (seated in center), Mr. Oldham (to Benson's left), and Mr. So (to Benson's right). Students included local evangelists from the Sham Shui Po church (Hong Kong) and the Mui Luk church. The curriculum and teachings were very much in the Stone-Campbell tradition. Mr. So taught a harmony of the gospels, relying heavily on J. W. McGarvey's "Fourfold Gospel," and emphasizing the "Divine pattern" for teaching and practices presented in Scripture. Mr. Oldham taught Old Testament history, including a study of the Mosaic Law and the Prophets. The purpose of this course was "to learn to know God." Mr. Benson concluded each session with a careful study of New Testament "doctrines and practices," with a strong exhortation to "restore the church to the New Testament standard." A continuing theme in the teachings and writings of the Canton mission team was the "restoration of New Testament Christianity."[11]

The dedication and contributions of the Chinese coworkers were essential to the progress of both the publication work and the evangelistic work. Mr. Oldham relied heavily on Mr. So to help with the translation work, and Mr. Ko led the evangelistic work at

---

11. Lewis Oldham, "Bible Study Course," 6.

Mr. T. W. So and his son, around 1933

Mr. and Mrs. Ko and daughter, 1930

the first street chapel established in the Canton Mission. Mrs. Ko worked among the women in the evangelistic work, as well.

In April of 1930, Mr. Benson commented that

> We now have by far the most capable and reliable Chinese coworkers we have ever had. We feel greatly encouraged, and expect the work to move forward with more definite progress.[12]

The Chinese coworkers' children also were a great help with their singing and participation at every Sunday School class. These coworkers' contributions would continue to be essential throughout the life of the Canton Mission.

12. George Benson, "Two Steps by Faith," 8.

Bensons' Furlough

In July of 1930, Mr. Benson resigned from his teaching position at the university and the Bensons returned to the United States on a much-needed furlough. They would return to Canton in April of 1932. The Oldham family remained in Canton, with Mr. Oldham directing both the publication and evangelistic works. The *Canton Christian* continued to be published, becoming the *Oriental Christian* in April of 1931.

The Bensons' furlough would be a busy one. After getting reacquainted with their families in western Oklahoma, and presenting their daughters (Lois had been born in Hong Kong in January of 1929) for the first time, the Bensons made their way to Chicago. Mr. Benson enrolled at the University of Chicago to obtain a master's degree in history with an emphasis in Oriental studies. At the end of the school year Benson wrote that "the past year has been more profitable to me than any other year I have ever spent in school."[13] This year of study gave Mr. Benson valuable insights into the history, culture, and people of China.

Benson family in 1929, Canton, China

13. George Benson, "Leaving Chicago," 4.

Following his graduation in August of 1931, the Benson family traveled around the Midwest, with Mr. Benson speaking at any church that would allow him to speak on the China missionary work. Funds were raised and important relationships established. The Cornell Avenue Church of Christ in Chicago, where the Bensons attended, became an important regular contributor to the Canton Mission work.

In the fall of 1931, the Bensons returned to Harding College in Morrilton, Arkansas. During the winter quarter Mr. Benson taught classes there on Chinese history, Oriental religions, and missionary methods. At least nine members of the missionary methods class expressed a desire to engage in foreign missionary work, and two young men committed to joining the Canton Mission in the fall of 1932. The *Oriental Christian* announced in May of 1932 that Lowell Davis and Roy Whitfield would be joining the mission team later that year. These two men would become outstanding workers in the China mission field for many years.

At the Canton Mission, the Oldhams assumed extra duties and became responsible for most of the mission work in the Bensons' absence. In March of 1931, Mr. Oldham, Mr. Ko, and Mr. So conducted a second term of daily Bible study classes, with four classes a day for eight weeks. The material covered included the book of Acts and various epistles, along with a number of doctrinal books, including *Sound Doctrine*, vol. 1, by by C. R. Nichol and R. I. Whiteside and "The Church of Christ," a tract by Leo Virgo. The students in the classes were the same as had attended the first six-week term. In May, working with their Chinese coworkers, the Oldhams were able to open a second chapel on Man Fuk Road on the East Bund of Canton. The combined membership at the two chapels grew to forty-six members, with many nonmembers in regular attendance, as well. During the year, some 350 meetings were held in the chapels.[14]

The literature work continued with the publication of 3,000 copies of *The Defender*, a Chinese magazine written to "declare the whole counsel of God," and to outline the "New Testament

---

14. Grace Oldham, *Things Chinese*, 33.

order."[15] The publication team also began the job of translating and publishing J. W. McGarvey's *Commentary on Acts*. Thousands of pages of gospel literature were published and distributed during the year. Mr. Oldham presented a series of lessons on the existence of God at both the Tung Shan Fan and Man Fuk Road Churches of Christ during the months of March and April 1931. These lessons were compiled into a book, *Is There Really a God?*[16] that was later published in Canton in 1932. In October of 1931, Mr. Oldham announced that J. W. McGarvey's *Commentary on Acts* had been published in Chinese. A sample page of the commentary appears below, depicting a baptismal scene from Acts chapter 2.

15. Lewis Oldham, "Growth of the Canton Work," 9.
16. Lewis Oldham, *Is There Really a God?*

Establishment of the Canton Mission

Page 28 of McGarvey's *Commentary on Acts*, depicting a scene from Acts chapter 2, with the heading "Biblical Pattern for Baptism."

The commentary was of high quality both in content and in construction. The book was later recognized as one of the best Christian publications in all of China at that time.[17]

---

17. Lewis Oldham, "Commentary on Acts in Chinese," 7.

In July of 1931, the *Oriental Christian* published a letter of great significance from the Morrilton, Arkansas, Church of Christ elders. Both the Benson and Oldham families had been "sent out" by this church. In the letter, the elders outlined and gave their support to the threefold program that had been developed by the Canton Mission team. They noted that the Bensons and Oldhams desired to undertake a bigger program for the work in South China, and expressed their confidence that the threefold program consisting of literature work, Bible training work, and active evangelistic work would be adequate to that monumental task. They concluded their letter with an appeal for more workers and more financial support for the China mission field.

More Mission Work and Reinforcements Arrive (1932)

In February of 1932, a third term of the daily Bible training class began. The teachers were Mr. Oldham, Mr. So, and Mr. Lo. For nine weeks, the students and teachers carefully studied the books of Genesis, Exodus, Mark, Acts, and Romans, as well as some topical studies. While the classes of these three terms were sparsely attended, they provided a solid foundation for the Bible school work that would begin on a larger scale in 1933.

Upon the Bensons' arrival back in Canton in April of 1932, the Oldham family went on a much-needed furlough to the United States in May of 1932. In the Oldhams' absence, the primary focus of the mission team was the evangelistic work in Canton. The work included daily evangelistic meetings and Sunday meetings at both of the local chapels. A special campaign was held in the neighborhoods near the Man Fuk Lo chapel.

Work in the fall of 1932 was focused on points outside of Canton, including Ng Chuen, and relied heavily upon the Chinese coworkers for preaching and interpreting. Mrs. Benson resumed teaching her Sunday school class. The literature work continued on a smaller scale in the Oldhams' absence. Mr. Oldham's book, *Is There Really a God?* was published in July in Chinese, in addition to a few tracts being reprinted. Requests for literature published by Mr. Oldham's team continued to come from all over China.

Oldham family on furlough, 1933

Plans were made in the fall of 1932 to expand the Bible training program into a formal ongoing Bible school in January of 1933. The training program would consist of a three-year course in Bible study to acquaint the student with the entire Bible. Students completing this coursework would also be given work in Chinese composition, taught by Mr. So, to prepare the students to teach others. Men, women, boys, and girls would be encouraged to enter the school. The new school, named the Canton Bible School, would start in a rented building with hopes to expand it to the point of needing its own building.

A critical addition to the mission team was announced in October of 1932, the hiring of Leung Hoi Kit, a former Baptist, to work as a teacher and preacher. Mr. Leung was asked to study at the Bible school for a time starting in January of 1933, to "learn the way more accurately."[18] He would continue to work diligently for the Canton Mission in various capacities, including Dean of the Bible School, until its closure in 1949.

H. K. Leung and family in Canton, 1936

The Canton mission team had anxiously awaited the arrival of Mr. Davis and Mr. Whitfield since the announcement of their

18. George Benson, "Present Activities in Canton," October 1932, 3.

decision to join the China work. Their coming was believed to be "essential to the effectiveness" of the present work of the mission.[19] Their arrival into Canton from Hong Kong by train on December 22, 1932, was welcomed with great excitement. Welcoming meetings were hosted by the Bensons and the Tung Shan Fan church. After a short Christmas break, work began in earnest in early January 1933.

Roy Whitfield (1906–1975) grew up in a country home in Ontario, Canada, and in 1929 he enrolled at Harding College. He chose Harding College because his father had been a classmate of Harding's President Armstrong many years before. He worked his way through college doing odd jobs and preaching on weekends. At Harding, he attended Mr. Benson's missions class, became interested in the China work, and volunteered to join the Canton Mission team. Following his graduation from Harding with an AB degree in mathematics, he spent five months traveling around Canada and the United States speaking about the proposed China work and raising support. He arrived in China with Mr. Davis in December of 1932 at the age of twenty-five. He continued in the work there until the Japanese threat forced the missionaries to leave in September of 1937.

Lowell Davis (1910–2007) grew up on a farm in west Texas, and in 1931 he enrolled at Harding College. At Harding, he also met Mr. Benson, became interested in the China work, and volunteered to join the Canton Mission team. He arrived in China at the age of twenty-two. For Mr. Davis, it was an interruption of his college work, which he would complete in 1939 at Harding, after his first term of work in China. He served more than twelve years as a missionary with his wife Odessa during three separate terms in China.[20]

---

19. George Benson, "Coming to China," 9.

20. Odessa Davis, *To China and Beyond*. Lowell (1910–2007) and Odessa (1911–2010) Davis spent three separate terms working as missionaries in China. In this remarkable book, Odessa chronicles their China years and nearly sixty additional years of ministry following their return to the states in 1949.

Lowell Davis (left) and Roy Whitfield, shortly after their arrival in Canton in December of 1932

Founding of the Canton Bible School (1933)

Upon their arrival in Canton, Mr. Davis and Mr. Whitfield quickly got to work. Language studies began immediately, for six hours each day. They were introduced to the mission's threefold program, and with the aid of an interpreter, each gave a series of lessons at the local chapels. The mission team was "greatly strengthened" by their arrival because they were both "young, capable, and full of energy."[21]

The mission team was full of optimism for the new year. Many tracts, several books, and a quarterly magazine were being published in Chinese. Both local chapels were essentially now self-supporting, and plans were being made for the opening of a regular daily Bible school.

The Canton Bible School officially opened on February 16, 1933, with fourteen students in regular attendance. Eight of the initial students were young men and six were young women. Classroom study consisted of five hours of lessons daily, with

21. George Benson, "Present Activities in Canton," January 1933, 4.

additional outside work to fill the rest of the day. The studies were extended for an enrollment period of nine months, with a three-month summer break.

First Class of the Canton Bible School, February 1933

The Bible school curriculum consisted of Bible as the main subject, along with Chinese reading, grammar, and composition. It would eventually be expanded to include church history, comparative religions, geography of Palestine, logic, philosophy, psychology, sociology, and English.[22] Another two hours a week were reserved for training in vocal music. The teachers, seated from left to right in the photo, were Mr. Leung, Mr. Whitfield, Mr. Benson, Mr. Davis, and Mr. So.

The original Bible school was housed in a very inconvenient old building on a narrow street in a busy section of Canton. Lighting and ventilation were both very poor, and the need was urgent for a permanent, suitable location for the Bible school work. A permanent location was also desired to house the literature work. The Bible school was moved into better rented quarters in September for the fall quarter, but fundraising for the construction of a new building for the school began immediately.

The Oldham family was on a furlough in the United States that would last until February of 1935. While there, Mrs. Oldham

22. George Benson, "Curriculum," 4.

underwent major abdominal surgery that required significant recovery time. But their work for China continued. During February and March of 1933, Mr. Oldham visited thirteen churches in and around Nashville, Tennessee, and delivered more than thirty messages regarding the China work.

In the June 1933 *Oriental Christian*, it was noted ominously that the Japanese invasion into Manchuria in northern China was a full 1200 miles to the north of Canton, and that the invasion "should have no influence upon our present undertaking."[23]

Simultaneous to the opening of the Canton Bible School, the mission team opened the Canton English Finishing School in February of 1933. The finishing school was designed to attract the upper classes of Chinese society, who already knew some English. A basic English examination was given, and only those students with some proficiency in English were accepted.[24] The goal was to attract these same students to the Bible school for religious teachings that were taught in more advanced English. Although it started out small, by the end of the year over one hundred students were enrolled in the English Finishing School. Mrs. Benson was the main teacher, teaching twenty-four hours each week. Mr. Whitfield taught twenty hours a week and Mr. Davis taught ten hours a week in addition to their preaching work at the local chapels.

23. George Benson, "Japanese Invasion," 5.
24 George Benson, *Missionary Experiences*, 87.

Congregants of the Kau Yuk Road Church of Christ

The above photo shows a portion of those who attended worship at the Kau Yuk Road chapel in December of 1933. Seated in the front row is Mrs. Benson's Sunday school class, including her daughters Ruth and Lois. The regular attendance at each chapel was around fifty for Sunday worship. A typical Sunday began with a Bible class meeting at 8 a.m., included several meetings at the chapels during the day, and ended with a night meeting at the chapel that began around 8 p.m.[25]

Mr. Davis made great progress in the spoken language and was able to make a short public speech in Chinese by September of 1933. By the end of October, he was able to preach a full sermon in Cantonese after only ten and a half months in the field.[26] Mr. Whitfield excelled in the written language, and was soon able to write more characters than any of the missionaries in the Canton Mission. He was also given responsibility for overseeing the boys'

25 Roy Whitfield, "How we Spend our Sundays," 2.
26 George Benson, "Renew," 4.

dormitory, which was part of the new rented quarters of the Bible school, opened in September.

Mrs. Benson and one of the Bible school girls regularly visited with neighbors around the nearby chapel, distributing tracts to the adults and picture cards to the children, taking their message into the local homes whenever possible. When they were not invited into homes, they went into shops along the street wherever they saw "open doors and idle people."[27]

Typical street scene in Canton, with a barber and incense candlemaker working in the foreground and modest apartment housing in the background

27. Sallie Benson, "Children's Page," July 1933, 6.

With Sunday schools, daily Bible school, English school, evangelistic work and Chinese publication work, everyone in the Canton Mission had plenty of work to do. By the close of 1933, all of the men were teaching and preaching, and Mrs. Benson was teaching, visiting the neighborhoods, and writing for the *Oriental Christian*.

Canton Mission Work Expands (1934)

By January of 1934 enough money had been raised to buy land for the Bible school building and the mission team was searching for a suitable location. Much more money was needed to construct the building. Mr. Benson, in an appeal for funding, wrote that "a country with 400,000,000 people must have at least one school in which to teach people the Word of the Lord, in an undenominational sense."[28] A permanent location for the building was found and purchased in April, at the northeast edge of Canton, in a rapidly growing school and residential area.

As Mr. Davis and Mr. Whitfield became more proficient in the language after a year in the field, the Canton Mission was in a position to expand outward. Mr. Davis began a new "country work" to take the message into the local villages around Canton. This work came with great difficulties, as the living conditions were more primitive and local opposition was at times more intense than in Canton. Mr. Whitfield began a program of "street preaching" in Canton, renting storefronts in different parts of the city and preaching every night for a couple of months at a time. He was by this time able to deliver a sermon without assistance from an interpreter.[29] The children who happened into one of these meetings were taught by young Chinese women from the Bible school. As of August, about twenty people had been baptized as a result of the street preaching work.

The Bible school opened for its second semester in February, with sixteen students enrolled for the daily classes, a slight

---

28. George Benson, "China Sunday," 4.
29. George Benson, "This and That," 4.

increase in enrollment from the previous semester. However, the school was being held in "very unsatisfactory" rented quarters, and $5,000 was needed to build a "suitable building of our own."[30] Fundraising for the new Bible school building continued in earnest in June of 1934. An appeal was made to individuals, as well as church groups, to become a member of the Bible school "Honor Roll" by donating $100 toward the construction of the new building. The Bible school enrollment increased to twenty-seven for the fall term of 1934, the largest class to date. Sixteen of the students were in the advanced class, with ages ranging from fourteen to twenty years. As the knowledge of the language and knowledge of the Chinese people increased, the teaching also continued to improve. Mr. Benson wrote regarding the Bible school work, "I cannot recall any previous work that gave me more genuine satisfaction."[31]

After searching for a suitable place to begin the country work, Mr. Davis decided to start work at Pong Woo, a village of about 10,000 people, located twelve miles north of Canton. Proximity to Canton was important, as assistance in the village work would often come from the Canton Mission. Mr. Davis was accompanied in the work by his language teacher Mr. Lo, who assisted in preaching and interpreting.

Until Mr. Davis's arrival, there had been no Christian chapel in Pong Woo. The initial meetings in Pong Woo went well, with about thirty of the Christians from Canton in attendance to lend support. On the third day of the meetings, however, a mob formed to prevent people from entering the chapel. The mob continued to grow, and Mr. Davis was threatened with physical violence. Eventually the local authorities sent out soldiers to investigate and restore order. Mr. Davis showed great courage, and plans were soon made to expand the evangelistic work to other villages in the district. The village work included preaching, distributing tracts, and meetings in homes whenever possible. A special women's meeting was also conducted, with help from the Bible school's women students.

30. George Benson, "Bible School Work," 1.
31. George Benson, "Bible School Building," 2.

Unfortunately, opposition at Pong Woo returned in the form of additional mob intimidation. People were again prevented from entering the chapel and the mob threatened to boycott any shop owner who came to the meeting. The government again provided temporary protection by sending soldiers for two weeks, but the problem recurred as soon as the soldiers left. Mr. Davis decided to return to Canton for a couple of months to allow time for favorable conditions to return to the village. During this time, he joined Mr. Whitfield in the street preaching work. In October, Mr. Davis returned to the village work in Pong Woo, where he found a more receptive audience, and some of the prior Christian converts willing to help with the work.

In September of 1934, Lowell Davis and Odessa White announced their engagement at a meeting of the mission team. Miss White had entered the mission field of China in September of 1933, joining the Hong Kong Mission. She had studied at the Portland Christian School in Louisville, where she was influenced for mission work by the teaching of R. H. Boll. In Louisville, she met the Broaddus family, who asked her to go to China with them. In Hong Kong, she studied the Chinese language while teaching English at a Chinese school. While there she worked with the Broaddus family and Elizabeth Bernard and her mother, Estella. When the Bernards moved to work in Loi So near Canton, Odessa moved with them. The village of Loi So was chosen as the first step in Elizabeth Bernard's plan to do medical missions work among the Chinese. Her nurse's training qualified her to do first-aid work as well as help with minor diseases and skin problems. She handled as many as twelve cases a day, and rarely had a day with no cases. Often her patients listened to her Christian message. Elizabeth wrote that "everyone who comes gets some gospel as well as medical aid."[32] It was in Loi So that Odessa met Lowell Davis, who visited to lead some of the Sunday worship assemblies.

---

32. Bernard, "Dear Friends," 7.

Elizabeth Bernard and her mother, Mrs. Estella Bernard

In August of 1934, the *Oriental Christian* published letters of commendation and support for the establishment of the new Bible school. James Cox, president of Abilene Christian College wrote:

> You are doing a most wonderful thing in establishing this school. It is the very best way to spread Christianity over there. I am certainly thankful to our Heavenly Father that you are doing this great work for the cause of New Testament Christianity.[33]

The construction of their own school building was viewed as a significant "forward step." The mission team believed that the planned facility could serve as a "cornerstone" for all of the Churches of Christ mission work in South China.[34] In September, the English Finishing School was moved to within a twenty-minute walk of the Bible school's location to accommodate the teachers who taught at both schools on the same day. The Bensons rented a large house one block from the Bible school location, and it included space for a girl's dormitory on the second floor. These

33. George Benson, "Honor Roll," August 1934, 3.
34. George Benson, "Honor Roll," June 1934, 2.

two moves served to effectively make the new Bible school building the work center of the Canton Mission.

House rented by the Bensons near the Bible school

The missionaries at this time were extremely optimistic regarding the future work of the Canton Mission and possibilities for expanding the work throughout all of China. Mr. Benson wrote an article "How to Accomplish the Impossible,"[35] in which he outlined an aggressive strategy for taking the message to the major centers of every province in China within a generation. The Canton Mission was just the beginning.

---

35. George Benson, "How to Accomplish the Impossible," 4–5.

Canton Bible School building during construction in September 1934

The formal opening of the Canton Bible School took place on December 15, 1934, with great celebration. For the missionaries, it was their "happiest day on Chinese soil."[36] The two-story brick structure was 45' by 80', and provided a significant improvement over any prior facilities that had been used for the school. The new building provided clean, well-lighted classrooms, well-ventilated dormitory rooms, office space for faculty, room for the publication

---

36. George Benson, "Canton Bible School Building Finished," 2.

work, and a small (20' by 45') assembly hall. More significantly, it was viewed as a facility that was ideal for the training of workers and future leaders that would be sent out to evangelize China. The school was known as the "Yuen To" School in Cantonese ("Yuandao" in Pinyin), meaning "School of the Original Path."

Canton Bible School building before its formal opening in December 1934

One of the first events hosted in the new Bible school building was the wedding of Lowell Davis and Odessa White. The wedding was officiated by Mr. Benson, with Elizabeth Bernard as bridesmaid and Mr. Whitfield as best man. The Davises moved to Pong Woo to continue the work there together shortly after a brief honeymoon.

Mr. and Mrs. Davis shortly after the wedding ceremony

Work of the Bible School, English School, and School for the Poor (1935)

With the excitement of the new Bible school opening behind them, the mission team moved forward into 1935 with great optimism. A new missionary would soon be joining the team. In January of 1935, the *Oriental Christian* announced the engagement of Roy

Whitfield to Ruth Gardner of Santa Rosa, California. Roy and Ruth's courtship had been an unusual one. In the fall of 1932, Roy first met Ruth when he stopped in California to visit her brother on his way to China. They went out together a few times before Roy's departure, and Ruth agreed to write to him in China. Over the next three years, friendly letters eventually turned into romantic letters, and Ruth agreed to marry Roy and join him in the China work.[37] Ruth's arrival in Canton and marriage to Roy would take place in July of 1935.

With the Oldhams scheduled to return from furlough in February, the complete team would be in the field for most of 1935. Mr. Lau would join the team in the spring of 1935 to teach at the Bible school along with the other Chinese coworkers, Mr. Leung and Mr. So.

Spring Term of Canton Bible School, 1935

37. Prout, "California Girl in China," 10–11.

English Preparatory School, fall of 1935

The English Finishing School continued its work throughout 1935, attracting young middle-class and upper-class Chinese eager to learn English. Soon after her arrival in Canton, Mrs. Whitfield became a regular teacher at the English school, joining Mrs. Benson, Mrs. White, and Miss Bernard.

The fundraising effort to pay for the new building continued successfully into 1935. As of January, forty-eight "honor roll" donors had each pledged to contribute $100. Twelve more honor roll donors were needed to bring the total amount pledged to $6,000, the amount needed to completely pay for the building, including additions. Improvements to the facility were already underway, with the construction of a kitchen and dining room outside the school building.

A view inside the Bible school chapel. It was equipped with hardwood furniture, a concrete baptistry, and seating capacity for around 150

Bible school kitchen, behind the main building

Dining hall and basketball court, behind school building

Small dining area inside the Bible school building

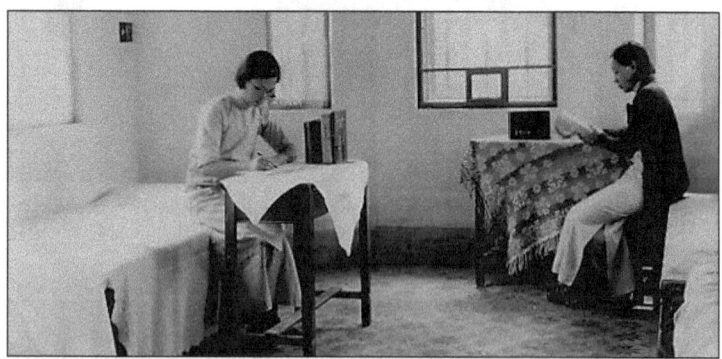

Girl's dormitory room, inside the Bensons' house

Establishment of the Canton Mission

In February, the Oldhams were welcomed back to Canton after nearly three years away on furlough. The church had a welcome meeting with numerous speeches on the importance of the publication work that Mr. Oldham led. Attention was given to the fact that these publications had resulted in churches changing their practices to conform more closely to "New Testament standards," free of man-made creeds and names.[38] In the April 1935 *Oriental Christian*, Mr. Oldham wrote an article stressing the importance of the Chinese publication work as an effective and cheap way to send the message, and "prepare the soil" for future growth.

The spring term of the Bible school opened with an enrollment of forty. As the students matured both in age and knowledge, they were able to contribute in significant ways. Two of the students were advanced enough to work with the Davises and Bernards in the country work in 1935. Others were able to teach Bible classes for the children. The Canton Bible School had not been designed to be a "preacher factory,"[39] but as a training center for all kinds of church work such as this. The desire was that Chinese from all professions know the message of the Bible, to take it with them to support the work of churches throughout every province of China.

After a summer break, the fall term of the Canton Bible School opened with an enrollment of forty-five students. Both Lewis and Grace Oldham were back as teachers, along with Mr. and Mrs. Benson, Mr. Leung, Mr. So, and Mr. Lau. The majority of the students were junior high level, with a small group at senior high level. About a fourth of the students were young women.

Mr. and Mrs. Davis continued the country work at Pong Woo. Odessa reported that the people were becoming friendlier and more interested than they had been for some time.[40] The difficult country work at this time consisted of trying to establish friendships and win the confidence of the villagers. Despite their best efforts, however, the work at Pong Woo never developed further. Although some friendships were established, their message

---

38. Lewis Oldham, "Back Home Again," 3.
39. George Benson, "Canton Bible School," May 1935, 1.
40. Odessa Davis, "Experiences," 3.

was never well received. In March, the Davis family moved their village work to Chan Tsuan, about two hours by boat southwest of Canton. It was a larger city of around 200,000, but with many small villages within walking distance. There the Davises joined Elizabeth Bernard, who had moved her medical missions to Chan Tsuan a few weeks earlier. They soon started a Bible class in their home, which grew to fifteen students. After some time of study, eight men from this class were baptized at the chapel of the Canton Bible School. Mrs. Davis and a Chinese woman from the Bible school opened a small school for children in the chapel at Chan Tsuan. The school met two hours daily, with an initial attendance of fourteen children, ages six to twelve. Mrs. Davis mingled with the Chinese children in a gracious way that allowed her to effectively teach them handwork and singing. The Chinese teacher taught reading, writing, and Bible stories. This ministry was free to the poor children of Chan Tsuan, and taught them many valuable lessons. Late in the year, however, the Davises moved back to Canton because of Mr. Davis's ongoing battle with dysentery.

Elizabeth Bernard extended her medical missions work to Canton, coming into the city each Tuesday for several weeks to speak to the students of the Bible school on the subject of health, including first aid and commonsense ways to care for one's body. In November of 1935, Elizabeth and her mother, Mrs. Estella Bernard, moved into Canton, where conditions would be easier for Estella.

Earlier in the year, Mr. Whitfield had established an important new work within the Canton Mission, a school for the poor. The English Finishing School and the Bible school had attracted students mostly from the middle and upper classes of the region. However, the neighborhoods around the Bible school had many poor children who had no chance to learn to read and write. Some of the best students from the Bible school wanted to serve in the local community and conceived of the idea of a school for the poor. To facilitate this program, Mr. Whitfield raised the funds and had a "mat-shed" building constructed on a vacant lot near the Bible school. Many of the students of the new school lived in houses made of this same inexpensive construction.

School for the Poor, Canton, China, 1935

Neighborhood near the Canton Bible School, 1935

The photo above shows around thirty children from the neighborhood in the front row with eleven student-teachers from the Bible school in the back row. The school for the poor became part of the Canton Mission's evangelistic work, as the children and their families were introduced to the Christian message. On Sunday morning, two of the Bible school students also conducted a Sunday school for the children with preaching for the adults. In addition to being inexpensive, the mat-shed construction was portable and could easily be moved to other neighborhoods to expand the evangelistic program.

In May of 1935, the Canton Mission opened its first evangelistic meeting in English. The objective was to make contacts with English-speaking Chinese who would generally be respected by the Chinese people as leaders. The meetings were held on Sunday afternoons, with an initial attendance of around fifty. The meetings were discontinued during the summer months, but resumed in September. The preaching was done by Mr. Oldham, Mr. Whitfield, Mr. Benson, and Mr. So. Follow-up work was done by Mr. Oldham in the form of printed announcements of future meetings sent to those who had attended at least once.

The wedding of Roy Whitfield to Ruth Gardner took place on July 23, 1935, at 2:00 p.m., in the chapel of the Canton Bible School, with Mr. Benson officiating.[41]

Wedding photo of Ruth Gardner and Roy Whitfield

---

41. Sallie Benson, "Gardner-Whitfield Wedding Solemnized," 1.

Ruth was welcomed as an exceptional partner in marriage for Roy and as a valuable addition to the mission team. She made good progress in the language and quickly made many friends in Canton. She was a very friendly, outgoing person, and was soon fitting in so perfectly that "nobody is conscious of her being a new missionary. We all seem to think of her as a vital part of the old force."[42]

By the close of 1935, the Canton Mission was at a high point, conducting a total of twelve evangelistic meetings each Sunday, with a combined attendance of around 450 people. Meetings were being held at the mat-shed building, the Bible school building, the YMCA, and in homes and chapels throughout the city.

High Tide for the Canton Mission (1936)

The Canton Mission Team moved into 1936 feeling that "prospects look good for 1936, and we all enter the new year with enthusiasm."[43] The team was as complete as it had ever been, with the Bensons, Bernards, Davises, Oldhams, and Whitfields all in the field at the same time. The invaluable Chinese coworkers were Mr. Leung, Mr. So, and the new teacher, Mr. P. W. Lau.

Mr. Leung was noted for being a "bundle of energy, and indispensable to the Canton Bible School, an excellent Bible student, and a very capable preacher and teacher." Mr. So was described as "a devout Christian, faithful to the word of the Lord, and dependable in every way, a natural-born teacher, much loved by the students." Mr. Lau, a younger member of the team, was commended for the "persuasive power of his preaching," and for having "great possibilities."[44]

The previous year had seen a record enrollment at the Bible school, the opening of the school for the poor, village work in Chan Tsuan, and new evangelistic work in the street chapels

---

42. George Benson, "Sister Whitfield," 5.
43. George Benson, "Brief Summary," 2.
44. George Benson, "Faculty," 3.

of Canton. The Oldhams had returned from furlough, and Ruth Gardner Whitfield had joined the team. Everyone on the team had contributed greatly to these successes, and as a result a total of forty-three people had been baptized in and around Canton.[45]

The Davis family had moved back into Canton to allow Mr. Davis a better opportunity to fully recover from the serious dysentery attack he had battled for much of the previous year. Two advanced students from the Bible school were sent out to Chan Tsuan to continue the village work started by the Davises. The Davises moved to the neighborhood near the Kau Yuk Road chapel and assisted with the evangelistic work in Canton during 1936. They opened small chapels, taught house to house, and Mrs. Davis started a Bible class for children. Mrs. Davis, Mrs. Benson, and Mrs. Oldham started a special class for women in April of 1936.

The Whitfields and a Chinese coworker continued their street preaching in local villages on Sundays, often attracting a crowd of forty to fifty adults plus children. Tracts were passed out to adults, and picture cards were used to attract the children. The reception the missionaries received depended greatly on the village. In one village, they were drowned out by a noisy group of young people banging on pots and pans, while in another village they were well received and returned for additional preaching.[46]

Miss Bernard's medical work and care of orphans continued in Canton during 1936. In June of 1936, the Bernards moved into a house near the Bible school. From that location, Miss Bernard would teach English at both the Bible school and the English school in the fall term.[47]

Mrs. Benson was engaged in teaching two English classes, one at the English Finishing School, and the other at the Bible school. The English school students were of "more or less means," while the Bible school students were from "more humble homes, but they are Christians."[48] She further noted that the Bible school

---

45. George Benson, "Brief Summary," 2.
46. Ruth Whitfield, "Village Trip," 5.
47. George Benson, "Bernards," 5.
48. Sallie Benson, "Classes," 4.

students were much more dedicated to their studies than the English school students. The English Finishing School was, however, attracting some students and generating interest in the Christian message by using the Bible in English as the text.

In May of 1936 it was announced that the Benson family would be leaving the Canton Mission and returning to the United States, where Mr. Benson would become president of Harding College in the fall of 1936. The decision for the Bensons was an agonizing one, as they had fully intended to spend their lives in the China mission field. Two major considerations convinced them to answer the call for Mr. Benson to become president of Harding. First, the Canton Mission team was now experienced. The Oldhams, Whitfields, Davises, and Chinese coworkers So and Leung were all "trusted, tried, and faithful" workers. The Canton Mission would move forward in good hands.[49] Second, the mission team believed that the Bensons could do more for the China work with Mr. Benson working as president of Harding College. With firsthand knowledge of the China mission field, he would be in a position to influence the recruitment and preparation of future missionaries for China. Many more missionaries would be needed to take the Christian message to the other great cities of China.

Also, the invitation had come from Harding's President Armstrong, who had influenced Mr. Benson's life "more than anyone else."[50] After many prayers and tears, the Bensons accepted the invitation and began making plans to arrive at Harding College in August of 1936. Mr. Whitfield became president of the Canton Bible School, and Mr. Oldham became editor of the *Oriental Christian*, both serving in these capacities until the Japanese threat forced the missionaries to leave Canton in September of 1937. The Canton Mission's threefold program of literature work, Bible training work, and active evangelistic work would continue forward to advance Christianity throughout China.

Prior to leaving, Mr. Benson took a three-week tour of inland China, visiting the major centers to gain firsthand information

49. George Benson, "Announcement," 1.
50. Ibid.

regarding the prospects for future missionary work. As the Bensons drove out of sight of the Canton Bible School for the last time, Mrs. Benson breathed a prayer that the school "might be made the center of sending out the 'light' to all of South China."[51] Her prayer reflected the fact that the Bible school had become the center of the Canton Mission and could serve as a model for missionary work in South China.

In the July 1936 edition of *Oriental Christian*, Mr. Whitfield restated the vision of the Canton Mission, to "see churches of the New Testament order established as soon as possible in the leading centers of China."[52] It was part of his appeal for more missionaries to come from America to lead the work in the great centers of China until the churches established there could become self-sufficient.

During the summer of 1936, a special evangelistic campaign was held in Canton. A small building was rented near one of the main chapels, with preaching every night. Two of the advanced students from the Bible school assisted in preaching. Mrs. Davis and a young woman from the Bible school held classes for the children, teaching Bible stories and singing with them. Most of the listeners at the nightly meetings were those who happened to pass by and stopped to hear the preaching for a few minutes. Some of the listeners would return from time to time, and they were encouraged at the close of the meetings to come to the main chapel nearby. Eight of the young people from the Kau Yuk Road chapel volunteered their time and conducted a summer school to teach reading and writing to the poorer children of the neighborhood. Around fifty children attended the classes along with a few adults. Every session included a Bible lesson.

In the fall of 1936, the mission team decided that for the good of the Canton work, only one missionary family should go on furlough at a time. Both the Davis family and the Whitfield family were due for a furlough, having arrived in China at the same time in 1932. The Whitfields agreed to postpone their furlough so that Mr. Davis, who had been weakened by dysentery, could completely

---

51. Ruth Whitfield, "Excerpts from the Bensons' Letters," 3.
52. Roy Whitfield, "Vision," 2.

regain his health while in the United States. The Davises would return to the United States for a much-needed furlough in March of 1937, before returning for a second term in China in 1939.

The Bible school opened its fall term in September of 1936 with forty-nine students, the largest enrollment it had yet seen. Mr. Leung, Mr. So, Mr. Oldham, and Mr. Whitfield taught in the Bible department. Mr. Lau taught Chinese grammar, composition, reading, and other regular subjects in the preparatory department, and Mrs. Oldham, Mrs. Whitfield, and Miss Bernard taught English. The daily school for the poor continued under the direction of an advanced student from the Bible school, with Bible teaching on Sundays.

The largest class of the Canton Bible School, Fall Term, 1936

The Kau Yuk Road church had grown to the point that its building was no longer large enough to accommodate all those attending, so the regular Sunday worship was moved to the Bible school auditorium for the school year.

Kau Yuk Road Chapel in downtown Canton, November of 1936

The church, however, faced a problem with retention of new members. Under the old religions of China, there had been no regular time of worship at their temples, outside of the special religious holidays. This made the practice of attending regular meeting times a difficult transition for many of the converts. Visitation work to encourage attendance was also difficult, as visitation among the Chinese was unusual, and normally required a formal invitation.

As of the fall term of 1936, the missionaries were managing or teaching in several schools: the Canton Bible School, the English Finishing School, the American Children's School, and the "Schools for the Poor" in Canton and Chan Tsuan. In addition, special Bible study classes were taught for those who expressed interest during the evangelistic meetings. Mrs. Davis continued her work among the children, working with Mrs. Leung.

ESTABLISHMENT OF THE CANTON MISSION

Missionary Team, Fall of 1936. Photo includes the Whitfields, Oldhams, Bernards, and Davises

"Grandma" Bernard, seated in the center of the photo above, returned to the United States in December because of her health. She had battled pneumonia the previous spring and did not want to risk another winter season in Canton. Miss Bernard stayed in Canton, taking into her home as many destitute Chinese as she possibly could. She met a blind woman who had expressed interest in becoming a Christian at one of the evangelistic meetings. The woman had been blind from youth and had been forced to become a concubine to survive. Miss Bernard took her in and taught her hand work and braille, skills she had learned in the United States before leaving for missionary work in China. Mr. Oldham continued his publication work by editing and publishing the *Oriental Christian* and a quarterly magazine in Chinese, as well as thousands of tracts that were distributed prior to evangelistic meetings. He also served as a teacher at the Bible school and the English Finishing School, and was an elder and treasurer at the Kau Yuk Road church in Canton.

Canton Mission Faces the Japanese Threat (1937)

The year 1937 would be a very difficult one for the Canton Mission team, with a shortage of workers, and the looming war threat which would eventually force the closure of the mission in September of 1937.

In January, Mr. Whitfield expressed concerns for the year ahead.[53] The Bensons and Mrs. Bernard had left the Canton Mission in 1936, and the Davises would begin their much-needed furlough in March. These departures would leave the team very shorthanded during the upcoming year, with an acute need for additional workers. The Whitfields, Oldhams, and their Chinese coworkers, the Leung and So families, would continue on to the extent possible the publication work, the Bible training work, and the evangelistic work. From Harding College, Mr. Benson would continue raising funds and recruiting workers. The need for workers was a recurring theme in the *Oriental Christian* throughout the year.

In January, Mr. Davis and students from the Bible school had held evangelistic meetings in the work camps of those building a new railway from Canton to the coast. Attendance was mixed, with crowds ranging in size from ten to more than one hundred. The spring term of the Bible school opened in February, with an enrollment of fifty. The work in the schools for the poor continued, with more than one hundred regularly attending. In addition to learning basic reading and writing, on Sundays the students were taught hymns and Bible stories. This work provided great training for the Bible school students and generated interest in the families of the poor children attending the school. Mr. Whitfield, with help from Bible school students, held evangelistic meetings in Canton.

During the winter break, Miss Bernard and Mrs. Davis had visited Loi So, where they had previously worked in medical missions and evangelistic work. Finding no preacher in the village, Miss Bernard wished she could "transform myself into a preacher"

---

53. Roy Whitfield, "Who Wants a Good Position?," 2.

and stay there.[54] The blind orphan girl that Elizabeth had adopted made great strides during the year, learning to read the Bible in braille, preparing herself for enrollment in the Bible school. Mrs. Oldham taught English at the Bible school and conducted an American School for Children in her home.

In March of 1937, the Davises left Canton to begin their furlough in the states. They would live in Searcy, Arkansas, while attending Harding College and speaking at numerous churches regarding the China work. In the March *Oriental Christian*, Mr. Davis reflected on the four years of their work in China. His language work had gone very well, as he could speak in Cantonese and be understood on almost any subject. The very difficult country work had been disappointing, hampered by lack of workers and lack of funding. Good evangelistic work had been started in several villages around Canton, but no permanent work remained in the form of independent churches. The hope was that much-needed village support workers would come from the Bible school. Mr. Davis believed that additional funding and training of workers would lead to successful country work in the future.[55]

The Whitfields moved into the house formerly rented by the Bensons, and continued to use the second floor as a girls' dormitory. Every Sunday morning Mr. Whitfield conducted an English class in their home, for students from the Bible school together with students from the city of Canton. The goal was for the two groups of students to become acquainted, and to introduce the Christian message to the students from the city.

---

54. Bernard, "Traveling Interior," 3.
55. Lowell Davis, "Our Work in China," 5.

The Whitfields on the porch of their rented house, spring, 1937

In April, the Christian Literature Society of China recognized the publication work of the Canton Mission. McGarvey's *Commentary on Acts*, which had been translated by Mr. So and published by Mr. Oldham, received positive reviews in the society's national publication, and was offered for sale in its bookstore in Shanghai. Mr. Oldham and Mr. So continued their work to publish a church history book in Chinese. Given the scarcity of high-quality Christian literature published in Chinese, this work was very welcome.

In June, Mr. Whitfield wrote that the mission team was too shorthanded to attempt any major evangelistic work outside of the Bible school. Some evangelistic preaching occurred in the Bible school chapel with limited success, as well as smaller efforts at the chapels in the city. Mr. Oldham and Mr. Lau, both teachers in the Bible school, led these efforts. Mr. Leung and his family, working with several Bible school students, carried on some evangelistic work in local villages. Mrs. Leung led women's meetings throughout much of the year, and Mrs. Oldham and Mrs. So led additional work among the women.[56]

The spring term of the school closed in June of 1937, the last term of the Canton Bible School until after the war. It was a term with good progress in Biblical learning for fifty students, including the school's first graduate, Mr. P. Y. Lei.

Bible school commencement photo, June 1937

56. Grace Oldham, "Summer Activities," 4.

While not satisfied with the "smaller results" of the work in 1937,[57] the mission team recognized that they were "doing what they could," and were hopeful that with recruits from the United States, the work would thrive again. Additional graduates of the Canton Bible School, expected in the spring of 1938, would also be a big boost to the work.

The July *Oriental Christian* made the exciting announcement that Mr. and Mrs. Leslie Burke from Harding College had committed to joining the Canton Mission team in the fall of 1937.[58] Mr. Burke had been a student at Harding College for the previous five years, graduated with a BA degree, and had taught Greek at Harding for two years. Mrs. Corrine Whitten Burke also had a BA degree and had been teaching school for several years. Mr. Burke had attended Mr. Benson's class on "Practical Missionary Methods," where he was introduced to the China work. The Davises, while home on furlough, had also encouraged the Burkes to join the China work. The announcement of the Burkes' decision was welcomed with great enthusiasm and thanksgiving by the mission team. Their arrival was scheduled for October of 1937.

In early July of 1937, a clash between Japanese and Chinese soldiers occurred in Northern China. This was the beginning of the military conflict that would continue in China until the end of World War II, in September of 1945. Mr. Whitfield wrote in the August 1937 *Oriental Christian*:

> We feel that there is really no need for any scare of war here in the near future. However, we have observed that the trains and river boats are doing a rushing business carrying many Chinese people out of Canton to Hong Kong and to villages.[59]

The war rumblings, however, led the mission team to delay the scheduled opening of the Bible school until later in the fall. Many of the Bible school students had left Canton to return to

---

57. Roy Whitfield, "Doing What We Can," 2.
58. Roy Whitfield, "New Missionaries," 1.
59. Roy Whitfield, "War Scare in Canton," 5.

their villages to stay with their families because of the threat. Mr. So and his family had also returned to their home town.

As late as August of 1937, Mr. Whitfield was hopeful that the school could reopen in October. However, because of Canton's significance as a port city, it was a target for Japanese bombing, which commenced on August 31. The bombardment would continue on and off until the occupation of Canton, which began in October of 1938 and lasted until the end of the war. Because of the war threat, the Burkes were denied visas to travel to China, and they returned to teaching in Searcy.

Departure from Canton

The American consulate in Canton sent a letter to all American citizens in the Canton district on August 17, 1937, urging them to prepare for a possible evacuation of Canton. United States gunboats would be available to take US citizens to Hong Kong if an emergency evacuation was necessary, but it was recommended that they leave by ordinary means of transportation. On September 18, the American consul told the Canton missionaries to prepare to evacuate no later than October 10. Air raids were occurring three times a day and bombs had fallen within a short walk of the Bible school neighborhood. The windows of the Whitfield's house had been shattered by bomb blasts. The missionaries painted a US flag on the roof of the Bible school in an attempt to keep it safe from bombs and invading soldiers.[60] On September 23, the Oldhams, Whitfields, and Miss Bernard took the little amount of luggage they were allowed and waited at the American consulate building until they could board a departing ship. In the afternoon, they were able to board a British steamer and with the escort of a British gunboat, made their way to the safety of Hong Kong. From Hong Kong, the group's luggage was transferred to the American steamer *Andrew Jackson* in preparation for its departure several days later. The *Andrew Jackson* carried the Whitfields and Oldhams safely out

---

60. Grace Oldham, *Things Chinese*, 104.

of the war to Seattle.[61] Miss Bernard remained in Hong Kong with her adopted children, working with Miss Ethel Mattley and the Broaddus family.

Mr. Leung and a Chinese coworker remained in Canton, looking after the two chapels there as well as the Bible school building. They were also left in charge of moving the household items of the missionary families into storage in the building, so that the mission work could quickly be restarted from the school when conditions would allow. Mr. So returned to his home village, continuing to the extent possible limited translation and evangelistic work there.

---

61. Ibid., 112.

3

Japanese Occupation and War Years (1938–1945)

Christianity During the Japanese Occupation

BROOK DESCRIBES THREE PHASES of the Japanese occupation and its effect on Christianity in China.[1] The first phase, from 1937–1938, he calls the "Period of Military Assault." While the military assault brought substantial losses and terror into the occupied territories, the Japanese army tended to respect Christian churches and mission centers. During this phase, the missions were recognized as foreign property that should not be disturbed. Brook calls the second phase of the occupation the "Period of Accommodation," from 1938–1941. During this phase, the occupying armies continued to recognize the neutrality of missionaries, and allowed them certain liberties in an attempt to win their cooperation.

The bombing of Pearl Harbor on December 7, 1941, put Japan at war with the home nations of most of the missionaries. This fateful attack led to the third phase of the occupation that Brook calls the "Period of Subordination to Japanese Rule," from 1942–1945. During this phase, foreigners were removed from involvement in Chinese Christianity, and mission property was often seized by the Japanese army for its own use. Japan wanted to

---

1. Brook, "Toward Independence," 317–37.

unify the Protestant churches, but under Chinese leadership, with the hope of winning acceptance of its dominance in the occupation state.

The Japanese occupation resulted in physical destruction of mission properties, scattering of clergy and congregations, and the absorption of Chinese Christian leaders into the workings of the occupying state. A summary of the conditions was reported by a national organization called the Church of Christ in China (CCC) in early 1946:

> From the surveys made thus far, we find discouraging features, ruin and devastation, many ardent church workers have given their all and are no more, others have lost their homes or their possessions. Yes, a few, it must be confessed, have succumbed to the hardships and dangers and thereby lost their faith.[2]

Despite the gloomy report, optimism was found in the conclusion to their report. The CCC survey found that "when all is added up, however, the encouraging features far outweigh the discouraging ones." Western missionaries were once again needed in China, and conditions would allow their return, at least for a while. They were especially needed for the leadership they could provide during the difficult postwar years, and were called by Chinese Christian leaders to return.

Japanese in Canton

The Japanese campaign against Canton began on August 31, 1937, when bombers taking off from Taiwan flew across the East China Sea and struck Canton. By the end of September the Japanese were carrying out almost daily bombing missions against the city. In January of 1938, the Japanese seized the island of Sanzao, off the coast of China near Macau, to use as a base for the invasion of Canton. In May of 1938 an air base was completed on Sanzao Island, and was used to launch raids against Canton. Throughout

2. Ibid, 335.

Japanese Occupation and War Years (1938–1945)

the summer months and into September bombing attacks were increased in the Canton area, including bombs falling on the grounds of Lingnan University, the oldest Christian college in South China. After heavy bombing for several months, on October 21, 1938, Japanese troops arrived at Canton and seized the city with little opposition. By this time, most of the city's inhabitants had fled to surrounding villages. Others had fled to Hong Kong, under British control, or to Macau, under Portuguese control. The Chinese had applied a scorched-earth policy in Canton, and much of the city had been set on fire. The Japanese occupation of Canton would continue until the end of the war in September of 1945.

Letters received by the Whitfields from Mr. Leung and students of the Canton Bible School give a picture of their brave attempt to continue the work of the Canton Mission after the departure of the missionaries. In October of 1937, Mr. Leung wrote that the Japanese were bombing Canton several times each day, and that the "school and church work are nearly stopped here because so many people have returned to their villages."[3] Sunday meetings at the Kau Yuk Road church continued, but with very few people attending. Mr. Leung and two students continued to live in the Bible school building in an attempt to maintain possession of the building and to guard the household goods and furniture left in storage by the missionaries. The hope was that the conflict would be short-lived and that the missionaries would return to reopen the Bible school within a year. By the summer of 1938, increased bombings forced the closure of both chapels in the city and Mr. Leung and the two remaining students closed the Bible school and returned to their home villages. Most of the Chinese Christians from the mission churches went into free China and carried on the work as best they could. The location of the Bible school in a residential suburb of Canton apparently protected it from being destroyed. The building survived the bombings and was used by Japanese troops during the occupation. Following the close of the war, Mr. Leung found the school building occupied by Chinese troops. He was able to regain possession of the building

---

3. Leung, letter to Roy Whitfield, October 26, 1937.

from the Chinese government, and a contracting company was hired to make repairs at a cost of $5,000.⁴

Continuing the Work in Macau: The Davises Return to China

Upon their return to the United States, the Whitfields moved to Santa Rosa, California, where Mr. Whitfield had been asked to preach. The Oldham family moved to Seattle, Washington, where Mr. Oldham started work as an evangelist. Both families would continue to work as missionaries, but in California and Washington rather than in China.

On furlough in the United States since February of 1937, the Davises moved to Searcy, Arkansas, to continue their formal education at Harding College. Mr. Davis completed his BA degree in history at Harding in June of 1939, and the Davises made plans to return to China in the fall of 1939. They had maintained contact with Mr. Leung and Mr. So, and anticipated restarting the work with them upon their return to China.

The Davises, with their newborn daughter, Avonell, returned to China, arriving in Hong Kong late in 1939. Mr. Davis's first task upon arrival was to file a claim for damages on the Canton Bible School with both the American and Japanese consuls.⁵ He believed that the Canton Mission could be reopened once he regained control of the Bible school building. Because the claim could not possibly be settled without a long wait, in February of 1940 the Davises decided to move from Hong Kong to Macau to restart the work there. Macau was a Portuguese island colony near the coast of China that had not been occupied by the Japanese and was considered much safer than Canton. In Macau, the Davises, along with Chinese coworkers Mr. Leung and Mr. So, attempted to continue the work of the Canton Mission.

The work in Macau is described in letters from the Davises to family members and supporters, and in Mrs. Davis's

---

4. George Benson, "Canton Bible School Building," 4.
5. Lowell Davis, "Lowell Davis Letter," 136.

autobiography.⁶ In Macau, the Davises furnished a chapel for evangelistic work and a small school to continue the same work of the Canton Mission, on a smaller scale. Mr. Davis wrote that "we expect to have a good school," and that "the work at the new chapel is doing about as we had expected,"⁷ with good crowds expressing interest in the Christian message. With Mr. Leung and Mr. So assisting in teaching and preaching, the evangelistic work and the Bible school work progressed steadily into 1941. Because of the Japanese threat to Hong Kong, Elizabeth Bernard moved with her adopted children to Macau in the spring of 1941, while Ethel Mattley decided to stay in Hong Kong. Following the surrender of Hong Kong in December of 1941, Miss Mattley was interned by the Japanese in Stanley Camp in Hong Kong from January 23, 1942, until June 29, 1942. At that time, she was released from her internment, loaded on the ship Asama Maru, and within a day set sail for home.⁸

Odessa Davis and daughter Avonelle in Macau, 1940

6. Odessa Davis, *To China and Beyond*.

7. Lowell Davis, letter to family, October 28, 1940.

8. Janes, "Missionary Notes," 251. After her release, Ethel Mattley (1887–1970) returned to her home town of Deadwood, South Dakota. She became a popular local speaker, often telling the story of her missionary work and internment by the Japanese. She never returned to China, but continued to support missionary work through her church in Deadwood until her death in 1970.

While the Japanese decided not to formally occupy Macau, their troops went in and out of Macau at will, and in August of 1943 they sent advisors as an alternative to complete military occupation. As a result, the situation in Macau became more difficult for the missionaries. Mr. Leung and Mr. So had returned to their home villages in free China in March of 1942. The conditions soon became too dangerous for the Davis family to remain, and early in 1943 they made plans to make their way to free China. Coastal cities were under Japanese occupation, so travel into free China meant a trip through occupied territory into the interior.

The trip out of Macau and into free China was a perilous one for the Davis family, now with four-year-old Avonell and their eight-month-old son, Cline. The Davises and their party left Macau by boat at night to avoid detection by the Japanese gunboats anchored in the harbor.[9] After reaching the mainland, the party traveled through the night on foot until they reached the West River where a boat was waiting to take them to free China. Traveling by boat, by bus, and on foot, the Davis family and Miss Bernard eventually reached Kweilin, about three hundred miles into the interior of China. In Kweilin was an airbase used by the US Army's 14th Air Force in support of China's defensive war against Japan from June of 1942 until November of 1944. The Davises spent roughly a year in Kweilin, living on a boat like the one in the photo below.

Sampan Boat along the Pearl River in Canton

9. Odessa Davis, *To China and Beyond*, 48–53.

Japanese Occupation and War Years (1938-1945)

In addition to a small amount of money received from their supporting church in the United States, the Davises survived by selling homemade candy and cookies to the troops. When the approaching Japanese threat became too great in June of 1944, the Davises were flown out of Kweilin to an airfield in Kunming, located in western China. From there, the Davises and Miss Bernard were flown over "the hump," the eastern end of the Himalayas, into Burma. From Burma, they made their way to India, and from there sailed to Australia. From Australia, they sailed back to the United States, arriving in San Diego in October of 1944. After visiting family and their supporting church, the Davises moved to Oklahoma, where Mr. Davis preached.

Davis family on furlough, 1945

Following the war, the Davises received letters from China requesting their return to reopen the Canton Mission. Mr. Leung had continued to preach in his home village, and many of the

The Field is the World

Chinese Christians from the mission work were still alive. Many places throughout war-torn China were suffering shortages of food and clothing, and Canton was no exception. The war had also left several thousand orphans living on the streets of Canton. Plans were made to return in the fall of 1946 to resume the work of the Canton Mission with a new emphasis on humanitarian aid.

4

After the War to the Communist Takeover (1946–1949)

Plans to Return to Canton (1946)

EARLY IN 1946 IT appeared that conditions in postwar China had improved to the point that the missionaries could return and resume the work of the Canton Mission. According to reports from the Christians in China, the school building was partly destroyed in the war, but the shell of the building was still intact. Repairs would be needed throughout the interior.[1]

Mr. Davis outlined the plans that were being made for the returning missionaries.[2] The Davis family would return to Canton and be joined by Frank and Earline Curtis in the fall of 1946, with additional families planning to join the mission team in 1947. Every phase of the work, including the literature work, Bible training work, and evangelistic work, would be renewed, and additional humanitarian work would be started. Early emphasis would be on relieving the suffering of the people brought on by the Japanese occupation. The program of relief would initially include the distribution of food and clothing and eventually the establishment of an orphanage for the homeless children of Canton. Plans were

---

1. Lowell Davis, "Davis Visits Family Here," 1.
2. Lowell Davis, "Gospel in China," 4.

made to expand the school facilities and programs to include kindergarten through high school, with college training to follow. Graduates from the Bible school would provide the leadership necessary to eventually develop self-sustaining churches in Canton and the surrounding area. McGarvey's *Commentary on Acts* would be republished in addition to the publication of other books, tracts, and a regular journal in Chinese. The program would be under the sponsorship of the College Church of Christ in Searcy, Arkansas.

The history of the Canton Mission during the postwar years until the Communist takeover in 1949 is largely told in letters from the Davises to their supporters in the United States and in letters sent between Mr. Davis in Canton and Mr. Benson at Harding College. Churches of Christ publications and the autobiography of Mrs. Davis also provide valuable insight.

Canton Mission Restart (1947)

A letter received by Mr. Benson from the American consul in Canton in January of 1947 stated that repairs of the Bible school building were progressing satisfactorily and that the building was in the possession of Mr. Leung. A letter from Mr. Leung stated that a small group of Christians had resumed meeting in the building and that it could be used to provide housing for the returning missionaries.[3]

The Davis family arrived back in Hong Kong on January 4, 1947, where they were met by Mr. Leung. After a short stay there, they moved to Canton to resume the mission work. At the first meeting with the Church of Christ in Canton, eleven Christians were present, with a number of visitors in attendance.

Mr. Davis immediately recognized the most pressing need was for relief work. Housing was critical, food was in short supply, and many orphans were seen roaming the streets. The United Nations Relief and Rehabilitation Administration (UNRRA) was at work in Canton, but it was plagued by inefficiency and corruption,

---

3. George Benson, "Canton Bible School Building," 4.

and was soon disbanded. Food and clothing were distributed to the poor, and plans were made to establish an orphanage. Plans were also made to soon ramp up the relief work in April through June, the time when the food supply was shortest and prices were highest. Additional repairs were made to the Bible school building and plans were made to purchase and repair a building that could be used as a girl's dormitory.[4]

Later in January of 1947, the Canton mission team was approached and invited to join the work of the Southern Commercial College (SCC) of Canton.[5] The SCC was a business and engineering school, with an enrollment of over four hundred students, that wanted to add Christian education to its curriculum. The mission team decided to accept the invitation and was given full control of the religious training, which was done at the Bible school building. Through this association, hundreds of students would hear and accept the Christian message over the next three years.

---

4. Lowell Davis, letter to George Benson, January 16, 1947. The letters exchanged between Mr. Davis in Canton and Mr. Benson at Harding College after the war indicated that Mr. Benson maintained significant interest in the China work. He advised the work at times, and was active in recruitment of additional missionaries and fundraising for China. However, the majority of his effort was in fundraising for Harding College and promoting his pro-Americanism agenda.

5. Lowell Davis, letter to George Benson, January 19, 1947.

Mr. Davis with Mr. Leung (far left) and Mr. Wan (far right), Dean of the Southern Commercial College

Mr. Davis with students from the Southern Commercial College, in front of the Canton Bible School

AFTER THE WAR TO THE COMMUNIST TAKEOVER (1946–1949)

The Davises were joined by the Bernards in February of 1947, and plans were made for Mr. and Mrs. Frank Curtis to join the mission team later in 1947. Attendance at the church meetings continued to increase, with Mr. Leung and Mr. Davis leading the worship. Mrs. Davis taught a men's English class at night, using the Bible for a text. It was a "great joy" for her to teach these men about God.[6] A building was purchased near the Bible school to use as a dormitory for up to thirty-six girls, and temporary housing was donated by the city of Canton to open an orphanage. The orphanage would initially take in twenty or thirty children, with more to be added as facilities became available.[7]

A midyear report from Mr. Davis indicated that much progress had been made since their return to Canton. A printing press had been purchased to help promote the evangelistic work through publications. In March, thirty people were baptized, and in April, forty-seven were baptized, mostly students and teachers from the SCC. Several of the students desired to go to America for further education, prompting Mr. Davis and Mr. Benson to begin making arrangements for them to attend Harding College.

Plans continued to move forward for the establishment of an orphanage in permanent facilities. Mr. Davis observed that "opportunities for work are many," and "I have never seen the people of China as open to teaching as they are now."[8] The most encouraging sign to Mr. Davis was the willingness of the new converts to join the work. In May, fifty-one new converts were added and the number of orphans increased to fifty. The printing press was up and running, printing tracts and a prospectus for the planned opening of the Bible school in the fall. Mr. Leung and Mr. Davis would be responsible for the religious education, with teachers from the SCC teaching the other subjects.[9] Plans continued over the summer for the construction of a permanent orphanage on a parcel of land purchased near the Bible school. The orphanage

6. Odessa Davis, *To China and Beyond*, 67.
7. Lowell Davis, letter to George Benson, February 28, 1947.
8. Lowell Davis, "Report from China," 11.
9. Lowell Davis, letter to George Benson, January 19, 1947.

would be built to house up to two hundred children and would include two dormitories, a meeting hall, classrooms, kitchen, and a dining hall. Overall prospects looked very good for future mission work, although Mr. Davis noted ominously that the Communists were making a "very strong bid" for China, primarily in the north of China.[10] The orphanage school building was completed in September of 1947, although it was used by the SCC until the end of the year. The Canton Bible School also reopened in September with more than twenty students.

Canton Mission Orphanage, 1948

Additional workers were greatly needed, and the mission team highly anticipated the arrival of the Curtis family. The Curtis family arrived in Canton, China, on October 10, 1947, where they joined the Davises in the mission work. They immediately began working, spending four hours each day learning the language. Mrs. Curtis and Mrs. Davis taught sewing to some of the older children in the orphanage and also taught them Bible lessons.

---

10. Lowell Davis, letter to George Benson, May 27, 1947.

After the War to the Communist Takeover (1946–1949)

Frank and Earline Curtis with infant child, 1948

Mr. Curtis taught Bible in English at the Southern Commercial College, assisting Mr. Davis who was also teaching Bible and conducting a daily chapel. Mr. Curtis had been recruited while at Harding College to enter the China mission field. He studied Chinese history and culture at Harding in preparation for this work, in addition to preaching at local congregations. His experience helping his father operate a farm in the Ozark Mountains of Arkansas would also prove valuable to the Canton Mission work.

In December, Miss Sheung Yi Wan began a Sunday school for village children near the Bible school. Miss Wan was the daughter of William Wan, dean of the Southern Commercial College. She was a dedicated student and worker, and was able to attend Harding College after finishing her studies at the SCC. Another dedicated student, Mr. Tit Fei Leung, the son of Mr. H. K. Leung, the dean of the Canton Bible School, also was able to attend Harding College starting in the fall of 1949.

In a December letter to supporters in the United States, Mr. Davis reflected on the work of the Canton Mission during 1947.[11] The work had "done well" that year, with a total of 210 baptisms, including the president and 170 students from the Southern Commercial College. Two small printing presses had been purchased and were being used to publish a monthly magazine in Chinese, as well as tracts and Bible lessons. The orphanage at year's end housed fifty children, with plans to increase the number to eighty in the near future. The Bible school had also done well, with a number of students already preaching and directing songs. A separate class was being conducted to train preachers. A group of young people from the school, led by Miss Wan, had gone into the local villages to generate interest in a Sunday school. After five weeks, the attendance was at one hundred students. With the Curtis family providing much-needed help, overall prospects for 1948 looked good. The Communist influence in the north of China was thought to be no danger to the work in the south.

Continuing the Postwar Programs (1948)

The continuing program of the Canton Mission for 1948 was outlined in a January article written by Mr. Davis for supporters of the China work.[12] Postwar China was viewed as a nation that had "thrown open her doors" to the Christian message. An evangelistic program would continue, with the goal to establish new congregations in other major centers. The Canton Bible School would continue to prepare Chinese students to teach their own people. Teaching a Bible curriculum at other schools in the city would continue to provide great opportunity to the extent personnel were available to teach. The orphanage would expand to give as many children as possible a home and a Christian education,

---

11. Lowell Davis, letter to supporters, December 6, 1947.
12. Lowell Davis, "Open Door in China," 3.

and the publication work would continue using the mission's own printing press.

In a January letter to Mr. Benson,[13] Mr. Davis expressed hope that additional workers from the United States could join the team in the fall of 1948. The programs were expanding to the point that additional workers were needed for the Bible school, the orphanage, and the publication work. Thirteen students from the Commercial College were baptized in February, and the Bible school was expected to open in the spring term with about fifteen students. In February, a special six-day Bible study was taught for fifteen of the local college teachers.

Senior Class of the Southern Commercial College, 1948

The Curtis family was doing very well in learning the language, able to carry on short conversations in Chinese. They were also learning the Chinese culture, and were well on their way to becoming valuable workers in the Canton Mission. Their first child was born on March 27, 1948.

At the orphanage, Mr. Curtis began taking care of seven milking cows, with hopes of expanding the herd to provide milk for all the children and the missionary families. A few pigs were

13. Lowell Davis, letter to George Benson, January 21, 1948.

purchased for the orphanage for breeding purposes, and plans were also made to operate a small sixty-acre farm. The desire was to make the orphanage as nearly self-supporting as possible.[14]

Mr. Curtis tends the milking cows, 1948.

Frank and Earline Curtis at the orphanage, 1948.

The Communists in the north of China were beginning to move. In April, the Davises were told by American officials in

14. Lowell Davis, letter to George Benson, June 22, 1948.

AFTER THE WAR TO THE COMMUNIST TAKEOVER (1946–1949)

Canton that the north would almost all be lost, but that conditions in the south were still very good. The Davises remained optimistic regarding the work of the mission. In June, South China was still peaceful and moving forward with its reconstruction efforts.[15]

By early May, forty-eight people had been baptized as a result of the mission work. Teaching continued at the SCC, but teaching Bible at other schools in the city would not be possible without additional workers in the field. Mr. Davis's focus was management of the orphanage as well as local preaching and evangelistic church work. Plans were made to turn the management of the Bible school over to Mr. Leung in the fall of 1948, with Mr. Leung and Mr. Davis carrying the teaching load. Mrs. Davis and Elizabeth Bernard taught English classes, using the Bible as the textbook.

The printing work was reported as going well during the summer of 1948. A monthly magazine was published and plans were made to publish special tracts for the summer evangelistic work. This work, including a Vacation Bible School, was planned for July, when the Bible school would be closed. Mr. Davis reported that "there are opportunities for any kind of work or worker." The greatest opportunity continued to be with the students at the SCC, although additional workers were also needed for the Bible school and orphanage.[16]

In September of 1948, Mr. Davis reported that the Bible school had experienced an unexpected increase in enrollment. Forty-four new students had enrolled for the fall term, with six of them at the high school level and thirty-eight at the college level. Space at the Bible school was being shared with the SCC, so a small temporary building was constructed behind the Bible school to accommodate the overflow of students. The decision was made to limit future enrollment at the Bible school to fifty students.

The orphanage had also increased to seventy children for the fall. Mr. Curtis took on additional teaching responsibilities at the orphanage in addition to his language studies. Plans were being made to open a high school for the children of the orphanage in

15. Ibid.
16. Ibid.

the fall of 1949. In October, Mr. Davis reported that plans had progressed to open a farm for the orphanage. A plot of land that could be purchased had been found a short walk from the orphanage. Plans were being made to purchase a tractor for the farm.

In early November of 1948, Mr. Davis wrote that "the political situation has deteriorated appallingly in the past week."[17] It was believed that within three months the entire country would be controlled by the Communists. While the missionaries did not yet fear for their safety, plans were made to evacuate to Hong Kong on short notice. Economic conditions were also deteriorating, with prices increasing so rapidly that much of the work of the Canton Mission would have to be scaled back or stopped completely.

In areas of China where the Communists had taken over, the missionaries were being treated unfavorably, and most missions had removed their workers. Many missionaries from the north and central regions were moving to Canton and Hong Kong to await further developments. Mr. Davis cancelled all proposed expansion of the mission work, and made plans to sell off all that might be looted should the mission be forced to close. Work at the orphanage was scaled back. Children with known relatives were returned to those homes, and no new children were accepted by the orphanage. Work at the Bible school was also scaled back as many students returned to their families in local villages.[18]

The American consul sent out a warning that anyone who could not stand severe hardship to evacuate Canton immediately. Mrs. Bernard made plans to return to the United States as soon as possible, although her daughter Elizabeth stayed with the mission team in Canton. Mrs. Davis went to Hong Kong to locate housing that could be rented in case of an evacuation, but the team was determined to stay in Canton as long as the work could be continued. In December of 1948, Mr. Davis wrote that the work was doing "fairly well," but the military and political situation was

---

17. Lowell Davis, letter to George Benson, November 8, 1948.
18. Lowell Davis, letter to George Benson, November 29, 1948.

"quite uncertain."[19] Remarkably the mission team carried on, making plans to resume work on the farm in January.

Final Year (1949)

Early in the year, Mr. Davis reported that many believed the political situation would become untenable in Canton within four to five months. In March of 1949, the Curtis family thought it best to return to the United States with their newborn baby, and the Bernards moved to Hong Kong. Many in the Canton Church of Christ developed Communists leanings, convinced that anything would be better than the present government. Despite this turmoil and uncertainty, the work of the Canton Mission continued on, at a reduced level.

Mr. Davis gave an overview of the mission work in a letter to supporters in April of 1949.[20] The Bible school had twenty-five students for the spring term, and several of the young men were preaching. Mr. Leung and Mr. Davis continued to teach. A class was opened for personal workers, with about twenty in attendance. Eighteen people had been baptized, including several from the orphanage, which was housing sixty children. The farm was under cultivation, the dairy was in production, and hogs and chickens were being raised. Mrs. Davis taught some of the older children in the orphanage how to sew. It was hoped that by the end of the year, the orphanage would furnish most of its own milk, vegetables, meats, and clothes.

The political situation, however, remained uncertain. In a poignant letter to Mr. Benson in April of 1949, Mr. Davis wrote:

> The situation here is not improving. It appears that Communism will over-run the country, but what the result will be to our work I do not know. They repeatedly affirmed religious liberty, but in some places this liberty has not been granted. Whether or not we will be under

---

19. Lowell Davis, letter to George Benson, December 28, 1948.
20. Lowell Davis, letter to supporters, April 8, 1949.

them or whether they will allow us to remain is still an open question.[21]

Reports coming out in July were that the Communists would capture Canton by August 15. This uncertainty made planning for the future of the mission extremely difficult. The remaining children in the orphanage were sent to be with relatives who could care for them. The Canton Bible School was closed, and the Davises moved to Hong Kong in September of 1949. The property that remained was taken over by the Communists when they occupied the city.

On October 1, 1949, Communist leader Mao Zedong proclaimed the establishment of the People's Republic of China, with its capital at Beijing, and the Communists entered Canton on October 14. General Chiang Kai-shek and approximately two million of the defeated Nationalists retreated from mainland China to the island of Taiwan in December of 1949.

After a short stay in Hong Kong, the Davises' sponsoring church in Searcy, Arkansas, called them back to the States. They sailed from Hong Kong on October 30 and arrived in Los Angeles on November 15, 1949.

---

21. Lowell Davis, letter to George Benson, April 11, 1949.

5

Conclusion

Remnants

EARLY IN 1949, SEVERAL students from the Canton Bible School were able to leave China to come to the United States to attend Harding College. These included Leung Tit Fei (Ted), son of the dean of the Canton Bible School, and Wan Sheung Yi (Shirley), daughter of the dean of the Southern Commercial College. Ted and Shirley became best friends at Harding and married in 1953. Upon graduation, they continued to live and work in the United States, where they raised a family, never returning to live in China.

When the Davises moved from Canton to Hong Kong in September of 1949, the formal work of the Canton Mission was essentially over, although remnants of its work continued on. The Leungs remained in Canton, and faced tremendous hardships because of the Communist takeover. The penalty for teaching Christianity even privately was harsh, and both Mr. and Mrs. Leung were imprisoned for attempting to run a small church in their home. Upon his release from prison, Mr. Leung sent word to Mr. Benson not to write him or attempt to send money because it would jeopardize his life. One former student of the Canton Bible School, Chun Hon Ching, returned into Kwang Sai Province and started a small school, collecting enough tuition to support his family. He preached at night in his schoolroom and was soon able to start a small church. He was ordered by the Communist government to do no more teaching either publicly or privately. He continued to preach in defiance of the government order, and was summarily shot in the street by a Communist soldier.[1]

By the close of 1949, Elizabeth Bernard had taken in fourteen orphans, taking care of some for several years and others for a short time. Mrs. Bernard died early in 1950 and was buried in Hong Kong. Elizabeth continued her work in Hong Kong until her death in December of 1971, and was buried in the same grave as her mother. The story of Elizabeth's remarkable life has been told in *Ah Wing's Elizabeth Bernard: Forty Years among the Chinese*.[2]

After the Communist takeover, Mr. So was able to make his way to Hong Kong where he began a small work, meeting with Miss Bernard and her family. He wrote in a letter to Mr. Benson in March of 1953 that a small house had been completed for his family to live in, and to use for worship every Sunday.[3] The Bensons were able to enjoy a reunion with Mr. So and several former students of the Canton Bible School in Hong Kong in 1960.

In 1982 Mr. Benson was able to return to China and visit Canton as part of a tour led by Professor Jack Lewis of Harding University. He visited the grounds of the Canton Bible School building and found the buildings being used as offices for the Communist government. The orphanage that had been operated by the Davises was being used to house a government school. Mr. Benson was able to locate Mr. and Mrs. Leung, still living in the neighborhood close to the school building. They visited for several hours, and Mr. Leung described the harsh experiences they had endured during the early days of the Communist takeover. He also told Mr. Benson that he continued to worship in his home with his family and a few neighbors that would visit from time to time.[4]

---

1. George Benson, letter to Ruth Whitfield, October 1, 1975.
2. Tune, *Ah Wing's Elizabeth Bernard*.
3. So, letter to George Benson, March 2, 1953.
4. George Benson, *Missionary Experiences*, 109–13.

CONCLUSION

Assessment of the Canton Mission

It is difficult to assess the accomplishments and lasting impact of the Canton Mission. The work was but a small part of the Protestant mission work in China from 1929 until 1949. Its accomplishments were more significant within the context of early Stone-Campbell missions, but the years of success and enthusiasm seemed to have been tempered by years of failure and discouragement. Reflecting many years later on the work of the Canton Mission, Mr. Benson wrote:

> What seemed for a long time to be years of wasted effort may prove yet to have been more productive than we even imagined possible. It would appear that a new day is dawning in China and that seeds, earlier planted, may yet produce an abundant harvest.[5]

China's Protestant community, which numbered an estimated one million members at the close of 1949,[6] grew to approximately sixty million members by 2011.[7] The growth since 1980 has averaged 10 percent per year, and if this rate continues, it will grow to around 160 million by 2025, more than in the United States. The presence of numerous house churches, not sanctioned by the government, probably make this number much greater. It may very well be the case that "seeds, earlier planted" by these and thousands of other dedicated missionaries have helped produce this "abundant harvest."

The work of the Canton Mission also helped establish Harding College as a leader in foreign missions among colleges in the Stone-Campbell tradition. The influence of Harding's first president, J. N. Armstrong, was significant, as the majority of the Canton Mission team was trained and sent to China from Harding during his tenure. George S. Benson, as second president of Harding, continued the tradition begun by Armstrong, and to this

---

5. Ibid, 107.
6. Miller, *Chinese Religions*, 185–86.
7. Pew, "Methodology for China," 97.

day, Harding University maintains a strong emphasis on foreign missions.

Assessing the history of mission work in China, the observations of Latourette can accurately be applied to the Benson, Oldham, Davis, Whitfield, Bernard, and Curtis families of the Canton Mission:

> The primary motives back of the missionary movement were unselfish. Selfish ones were undoubtedly there: the increase of the glory and power of a Western nation or of an order or a society, the desire for personal renown, and the urge to adventure. Missionaries were pioneers and were impelled in part, as are all pioneers, by a passion for achievement in a fresh environment. In the great majority of missionaries, however, the dominant motive had little of self: it was a feeling of obligation to share with others a message, a salvation, a way of life which the missionary believed of supreme importance.[8]

These missionary families went into China without knowing what awaited them there. They labored under conditions that were difficult at best, yet continued the work until it was no longer possible. They sacrificed greatly to deliver the Christian message they believed was so important. Their field *was* the world.

---

8. Latourette, *History of Christian Missions in China*, 824.

Appendices

SEVERAL ADDITIONAL TOPICS RELEVANT to the work of the Canton Mission are discussed in the appendices below. The discussion is intended simply to provide a basic overview of these important topics.

Appendix A

Operations of the Canton Mission

Fundraising

ONE OF THE MAJOR factors leading to the separation of the Churches of Christ from the other streams of the Stone-Campbell restoration movement was its opposition to missionary societies.[1] Alexander Campbell and other leaders of the movement opposed missionary societies because they believed mission work was the responsibility of the churches, not an organized society. Despite this opposition, Campbell allowed that churches working together in mission fields could provide a more efficient means of spreading the gospel, and was for many years the president of the American Christian Missionary Society. The Churches of Christ, however, firmly opposed missionary societies and any other organizational development outside the church.

Lack of a missionary society infrastructure made fundraising, recruitment, and training efforts extremely difficult for the early missionaries of the Churches of Christ. The approach to fundraising adopted by these missionaries included soliciting support from "living link" congregations, as well as funds raised and distributed by "forwarding agents," who volunteered to work as

---

1. Foster et al., "Missions, Missiology," 537–42. Foster discusses the controversy in a fair amount of detail, and provides a timeline of missionary organization within the Stone-Campbell movement from 1809 to 1996.

Appendix A

liaisons, collecting funds from supporters and sending them to the missionaries in the field.[2]

Despite this type of help from supporters at home, fundraising for the Canton Mission was piecemeal and inefficient, with the missionaries themselves left to do the bulk of the fundraising work. Most editions of the *Oriental Christian* included an appeal for funds, and the money sent by each donor was listed, regardless of the amount, in a subsequent edition, as shown below. Individual receipts and disbursements were listed for each missionary family, to maintain accountability for both the donors and the missionaries. The missionaries had no set salary, with support depending on how much money was received in a given month.

Forwarding agents did contribute to the fundraising efforts of the Canton Mission, notably Don Carlos Janes and B. D. Morehead. Both Janes and Morehead were regular contributors to the Churches of Christ publication *Word and Work*, often writing columns and soliciting funds in support of mission work. Janes worked as the treasurer for the Highland Church of Christ in Louisville, Kentucky, and Morehead was a former missionary to Japan who spoke at numerous churches over many years in support of missions. It was reported that in the first half of 1932 alone, he visited ninety churches, traveling over 12,000 miles.[3]

The Canton Mission also used special fundraising drives for specific needs such as the financing of the Bible school building. A special brochure showing the plans and need for the building was published and sent to supporters. The goal was to raise $5,000 for the construction of the school building. The fundraising drive sought fifty donors of $100 each, with the promise that each donor's name would be engraved in stone at the entrance to the school.[4] The building and grounds together ended up costing approximately $7,500, but the original goal of $5,000 was raised through this effort.[5]

2. Ibid., 539.
3. Morehead, "Among the Churches," 8.
4. George Benson, "Honor Roll," 1.
5. George Benson, "Payment to Be Made at Once," 3.

| October, 1936 | ORIENTAL CHRISTIAN | 5 |

FINANCIAL REPORTS FOR SEPTEMBER
Mr. and Mrs. Roy Whitfield

RECEIPTS:
Church, Forest, Ont.	$	4.00	Fairview Church, Detroit, Mich $	7.20
O.W. Gardner's Class, Santa Rosa, Calif		20.49	Church Sunday School, Erin Ont.	5.00
Mrs. Brittell's Class, Santa Rosa, Calif		2.00	Church, Hamilton, Ont	6.00
			Church, Cape Rich, Ont	5.00
A Friend, Amite, La		1.00	Church, Woodgreen, Ont	10.00
Ladies' Bible Class, Windsor, Ont.		5.00	John S. Whitfield	2.00
			Geraldine Rhodes	1.00
Mrs. E. Moore		1.00	Through Mrs. E.H. Franklin	2.00
Church, Sarnia, Ont.		4.00	Charles Erb	10.00
Young People's Class, Sacramento, Cal		2.00	Mr. and Mrs. Robert Neil	10.00
			David Neil	5.00
Beecher & Raymond Sts. Church, St. Catherines, Ont.		5.00	Winston Neil	3.00
			Total Receipts	$ 110.69

DISBURSEMENTS:
To Mr. and Mrs. L.B. Davis Personal Support	$	5.00
Mr. and Mrs. Roy Whitfield Personal Support		105.69
Total Disbursements ...	$	110.69

Financial report for September 1936 (OC, October 1936).

The Canton Mission was thus funded through a variety of sources, including small donations from individuals, larger sums raised by home congregations or forwarding agents, and special fundraising drives for the costly items. The missionary families never accepted more than was necessary to survive, with few luxuries. The generosity of supporters, giving from scarce means during the depression era, was equally notable.

Governance

The Canton Mission embraced the Protestant strategy, the so-called "Three-Self Movement,"[6] to build independence for the new Chinese Christians. The goal of this informal movement was to

---

6. Bays, "Growth of Independent Christianity," 308.

Appendix A

make Chinese Christians responsible for "self-management, self-support, and self-propagation" in the newly established churches. It had been a goal of many foreign missionaries in China since the mid-nineteenth century.

This goal presented significant challenges to the workers of the mission. A key purpose of the Bible school was always to develop leaders for the newly established churches, but the question of when to turn over leadership to a particular local church was still a difficult one. Turning leadership of the church over to the Chinese converts either too soon or too late could bring serious problems to the church.

Mr. Oldham wrote about this tension in the *Oriental Christian*.[7] The Chinese converts in general did not have the religious heritage of past generations of Christians, and they lacked the support of a strong Christian community. This in turn led the missionaries to believe they needed to hold onto control and direct all church affairs. Maintaining control for too long, however, caused resentment on the part of the Chinese Christians. The missionary was seen as nothing but a dictator, trying to run everything according to his own foreign ideas. The church was then viewed as a foreign institution on Chinese soil, and many local converts became disinterested and left the church.

Turning over control before proper leadership was developed also led to significant problems for a fledgling church. The danger was that immature leadership would lead the church into error in its methods of "government, edification, and support." The church would then depend on "unscriptural and questionable means of raising funds, periodical conventions, and super-organization" for its life. The church in this condition would stray away from the "pattern given by our Lord."[8]

Avoidance of these problems depended on several factors. The missionary had to be careful not to rely on traditions of the home church to guide decision making, but to appeal to accepted Biblical teachings to guide the decisions made and actions taken.

---

7. Lewis Oldham, "Some Missionary Problems," 6.
8. Ibid.

This approach made the church less of a foreign institution in the eyes of the Chinese converts. The other important factor was the development of capable leadership through teaching and training, with the stated goal of independence of the local church. This was a primary goal of the Canton Bible School, stated in a bulletin published by the school:

> In order to obtain safe church leadership, people must be taken young, put into a proper environment, and thoroughly taught the word of God. They should also, by practical experience, be brought into contact with every sort of problem that may arise in religious work, and taught by example how each particular problem should be solved. It is the aim of the Canton Bible School to provide this proper environment, the thorough Bible teaching, and the practical experience in actual evangelistic work. Before graduation the students are expected to do three years of classroom work, and to have one year of practical experience out in actual evangelistic endeavor.[9]

It was the desire of the Canton Mission to develop self-sustaining churches as quickly as possible. Yet several years of training were needed to develop leadership that would enable the infant churches to grow in a healthy fashion. The Kau Yuk Road Chapel began its work late in the fall of 1932. By the fall of 1936, it was largely self-sustaining, with Chinese elders that were "diligent in striving for the welfare of the congregation."[10] Evangelistic meetings were frequently held at the chapel, with special lessons taught by Mr. Leung, Mr. So, and Mr. Oldham and preaching done by Mr. Lau and Mr. Davis. The members were for the most part very poor, but the church was able to survive, using a rented building for meetings and rotating preaching responsibilities among its members.

While it was the desire of the mission that local churches quickly become self-governing, the governance and operations of the Canton Bible School always remained under the direction of

---

9. George Benson, "Aim," 4.
10. Lewis Oldham, "Kau Yuk Road Church of Christ," 1.

Appendix A

the missionaries. None of the Chinese coworkers were part of the school's governing body.

A constitution of the Canton Bible School was written in 1934 to provide for the ongoing governance of the Bible school. The original president and treasurer was Mr. Benson, and the original board of trustees consisted of Mr. Benson, Mr. Oldham, Mr. Davis, and Mr. Whitfield. The stated purpose of the school was to "give thorough and efficient Bible teaching and such other practical training as is necessary in order to build Christian character and to fit people for usefulness in the church of the Lord."[11] Guidance was given in the constitution regarding religious practices, hiring and firing of faculty, organizational structure, qualifications of board members, decision making procedures, duties of officers, and a process for amending the constitution.

Quarterly business meetings were held in the home of one of the missionary families. Each missionary would report on their work, including any successes or failures, with group discussion and possibly recommendations and motions following. Using this process, decisions were made regarding the ongoing operations of the Bible school.

---

11. George Benson, "Name and Object," 1.

Appendix B

Religion and Doctrine

Religious Background of the Chinese

DURING THE TIME OF the Canton Mission, China's prominent religions were ancestor worship, Confucianism, Taoism, and Buddhism.

With ancestor worship, worship was given both to ancestors and to a variety of spirits, including spirits of the mountains and rivers. The worship of spirits of ancestors was particularly prominent, with offerings including food, wine, incense, candles, and flowers. Ancient tradition taught that if sacrifices such as oxen, sheep, and pigs were not made to deceased ancestors, they would become homeless spirits wandering through the night, haunting the living. Ancestral spirits that were properly cared for became kind spirits, sending blessings of good fortune, health, wealth, success, happiness, sons, long life, and peaceful death to their descendants.[1] This worship was also a display of respect for one's parents and ancestors, a great virtue in Chinese culture.

Confucianism was primarily interested in social welfare and government, with the belief that the welfare of society depended on maintaining the principles and the practices of the ancients. A follower became noble by developing five virtues which were central to the Confucian school of thought: benevolence, righteousness,

---

1. Perkins, "Ancestor Worship," 11–12.

proper conduct, wisdom, and trustworthiness. The emphasis was on practicing these virtues, seen chiefly as an aid to a healthy society and good government. The teaching maintained that when all family relationships are in order, there will be order in society. The existence of God and man's relationship to God were not major concerns of Confucianism. The major concern of Confucianism was how to live your life properly, for the good of society and nation.[2]

Taoism was appealing to the Chinese because it emphasized personal freedom and harmony with nature. Like Confucianism, its chief interest was in the welfare of society. It did not rely on a complex system of ethics, however, but on simplicity and non-interference. Its teaching was highly moral, but was opposed to ethical codes. It encouraged self-forgetfulness, returning good for evil, the absence of pride, and peace of spirit as man's goal. The wise man was the one who "takes no action" that interferes with anything but leaves things alone. Such a person is in harmony with the "Tao," the source of all things that exist.[3]

Buddhism was introduced into China from India around the first century AD and developed into one of the three main religions of China, along with the older religions Confucianism and Taoism. The four "noble truths" of Buddhism were that life entails suffering, suffering is due to desires, it can be stopped if desire is stopped, and this can be done by leading a disciplined and moral life and engaging in meditation.[4] Salvation for the Buddhist was a message of peace, of escape from suffering and the endless chain of reincarnations. Buddhism did not reject the existence of gods, but it held that they were subject to change and for all practical purposes could be ignored. Buddhism was popular with the masses and often with the wealthy. Buddhist temples were numerous in China and there were sacred mountains, vows, and pilgrimages. Major effects of Buddhism were to greatly influence art and

---

2. Perkins, "Confucianism," 100–102.
3. Perkins, "Daoism," 117–19.
4. Perkins, "Buddhism," 47–50.

literature, to reinforce the native moral standards, and to give the masses some assurance of immortality.

The religious background of the Chinese at the time of the Canton Mission was thus the product of many ancient movements. While generalizations are difficult at best, certain features of Chinese religious thinking do emerge as characteristic. The Chinese of this time were usually tolerant on matters of religion, and in practice felt no sense of inconsistency in being a Confucianist, Taoist, and Buddhist, each religion filling its place in their lives. Converts to a new religion would tend to simply add in the new with the existing older faiths, as long as it served some useful purpose in everyday life.

Another significant feature of Chinese religion was polytheism. Divinities were numerous, some of native origin and some the contributions of other peoples. A different god existed for every aspect of Chinese life. There was a formally recognized hierarchy of "gods" that was modelled after the structure of the ancient empires.

The Chinese religions each taught a strong sense of ethics, with great emphasis on good conduct for the benefit of order in family, society, and government. Given this respect for ethics, however, there was no sense of sin against a personal God as found in the biblical writings. There was little sense of guilt and no sense of the release from guilt that is found in Christian teachings. There was no perceived need for a mediator between man and a personal God, and no perceived need for a redeemer. Righteousness arose not from any compelling relationship with God, but from a necessary regard for family, society, a genuine concern for the welfare of all people, or desire for a life of bliss after death.

Latourette (1929) summarizes his discussion of the religious background of the Chinese and the obstacles it presented for missionaries by observing:

> Any religion arriving for the first time in China would have no easy time in becoming established. It would find already in the field highly organized faiths with elaborate philosophies entrenched in the traditions and the

Appendix B

institutions of the people. If it could meet a real need and if it could tolerate the presence of existing religions, ideas and institutions, it might find a welcome. It would run the danger, however, of being absorbed and of losing its distinctive characteristics and even its identity. If, on the other hand, the new religion proved intolerant of native faiths and if its acceptance would involve any revolutionary changes in thought or in social, political, and economic institutions, *its path would not be smooth*. It would have to attack some of the outstanding features of the nation's life and thought and affect their destruction or transformation. This process would entail prolonged and extensive missionary work and even then might be unsuccessful unless other forces were to aid in the disintegration of the nation's life. Under the most favorable circumstances *the conquest of China by a new faith would be the work of centuries and of thousands of earnest agents.*[5]

Religious Commonalities and Differences

Christianity had some common ground with the ancient religions of China, but the many differences were profound. Like Buddhism and Confucianism, Christianity places much emphasis on ethical behavior. Jesus' teaching about the "kingdom of God," at least in part, parallels the Confucian desire for an ideal social order. The Chinese desire for social welfare depended upon man giving himself to the service of his fellow man, an ideal emphasized in Christian teachings. The Christian idea of vicarious suffering and salvation by faith in the sufferer is found in a branch of Buddhism, although "salvation" to the Buddhist meant a future life of bliss. All of the ancient Chinese religions spoke, in some form, of a life beyond the grave, an idea prominent in Christian thought. To the Chinese, then, not all the teachings of Christianity would come as completely strange.

---

5. Latourette, *History of Christian Missions in China*, 23–24.

Religion and Doctrine

The differences between Christianity and the Chinese religions were of course many, and were significant. The motivation for ethical behavior was very different. Jesus' statements regarding ethical behavior were based on the teaching that God loves each individual, and desires that each man love God and love his fellow man. Confucianism, however, did not view God as a personal God who loves individuals. Buddhism believed that gods, like men, were not permanent and were of little or no assistance in man's search for salvation. Buddhism and Confucianism also popularly practiced polytheism, while Christianity insisted upon one God. The Christian God was a God who sustains the universe, yet loves and desires fellowship with the individual man, an idea little known in the Chinese religions.

These differences would undoubtedly lead to the opposition of Christianity in China. It would have to find commonalities, where possible, with the ancient religions that had been in place for millennia. To attack ancestor worship, for example, would be an attack upon the most important social institution of China, the family. Christianity would need to show that its adoption would lead to a richer family life. Christianity would also be in the position of attacking many of the religious ceremonies, carried on by the state, that were an important part of the life of the local village or city. Christianity's exclusivism with respect to other religions and its rejection of polytheism would be a direct affront to the ancient religions. While many Chinese followed parts of multiple religions, Christianity could not blend in with the other religions without compromising its teachings.

Christianity would also meet opposition simply from the fact that it was foreign. The Chinese had great pride in their own culture and traditions and contempt for anything foreign. Christianity would also be opposed by the educated leaders of the long-standing religions of China, who feared losing their place in society if Christianity succeeded.

Latourette (1929) makes a further sobering observation regarding the challenge facing the Christian missionaries:

Appendix B

> Since Christianity necessarily runs counter to so much that is an integral part of Chinese culture . . . and has become identified with certain ecclesiastical and doctrinal systems that are alien to Chinese experience, it is obvious that *in China it can have no easily won triumph*. It can succeed only by bringing enough forces to bear and for a sufficient period to work a revolution.[6]

Canton Mission Theology and Doctrine

Given the religious traditions encountered in China, the missionaries often began their teaching and preaching with basic arguments for the existence of a single God and for the authenticity of the Bible as a revelation from that God.

Mr. Oldham gave a series of eleven lectures on the existence of God, presented in the Tung Shan Fong and Man Fuk Road Chapels in Canton during the months of March and April 1931. The lectures were compiled and published in both English and Chinese in a book entitled *Is There Really a God?*[7] For the lectures, he brought together a great deal of material on science and religion and evidences of Christianity. Working with several prominent Chinese scientists, Mr. Oldham developed scientific arguments for the existence of God. He contrasted atheistic and Christian thought, and presented historic and scientific arguments for the authenticity of the Bible.[8]

A sermon by Mr. Benson published in the *Oriental Christian* was a "fair representation" of how he introduced Christianity to the Chinese people.[9] The sermon began with the argument that nature was a powerful witness to the existence of a supreme being, God. It was the duty of this God to reveal himself to his creation, so a personal messenger was needed. The prophets of Israel and the miracles of Jesus pointed to him as the unique messenger of

---

6. Ibid., 44
7. Lewis Oldham, *Is There Really a God*, 1–37.
8. Ibid., 44–79.
9. George Benson, "God's Revelation," 2–3.

Religion and Doctrine

God. After suffering death and being raised from the dead, the messenger returned to God, but left a permanent record of his revelation from God. From this revelation, all nations would for all time have a knowledge of God and his will for mankind. Additional instructions were prepared for those who would accept Jesus as God's messenger, instructing them how to live in a way to please God.

Emphasis was placed on obedience to God's will, as interpreted from the Bible. The constitution of the Canton Bible School had a clear statement of purpose that reflected this philosophy:

> The New Testament is a full and complete guide in Christian worship and service. In matters of doctrine and practice it shall be the purpose of those teaching *"To speak where the Bible speaks and to be silent where the Bible is silent."* Undenominational Christianity shall be stressed, and Christian unity urged and advocated by a return to the Bible and the rejection of all man-made creeds and innovations.[10]

The missionaries' sermons, as they appeared in the *Oriental Christian*, emphasized an obedience that included "New Testament practices observed, and congregations built up after the New Testament pattern throughout China."[11] This teaching was very much in line with the dominant "pattern hermeneutics"[12] of the Churches of Christ during this era.

The evangelistic meetings held in Canton would typically last a week or two, with fundamental Christian subjects discussed every night. The subjects included an introduction to God, man's relationship to God, God's revelation, Christ's purpose for coming into the world, why men need Christ, how to obtain salvation, Christ and new life, and the judgment. Special Bible classes were offered following the meetings for those who desired to study more.[13]

---

10. George Benson, constitution of the Canton Bible School, 1.
11. George Benson, "Realities of Missionary Work," January 1931, 5.
12. Holloway, "Current State of Hermeneutics," 3.
13. Lowell Davis, "Evangelistic Meetings," 6.

Appendix C

Hindrances to the Work

THE MOST SIGNIFICANT HINDRANCES encountered by the workers of the Canton Mission included the language barrier, cultural and gender-based traditions, religious traditions in China, Chinese attitudes toward foreigners and missionaries, and the missionaries' own misconceptions and lack of preparedness entering the mission field.

The Language Barrier

One of the first challenges the missionaries faced upon arrival in China was learning the language. Cantonese was the prevailing language in the southern provinces of Kwang Tung and Kwang Sai. Outside of these two provinces, however, it was not spoken, as the official language Mandarin was spoken throughout most of China. Learning this tonal language was a great obstacle for each of the missionaries. The quickest learner was Mr. Davis, who was conversational in the language within ten months. Studying several hours daily, it took the others a full year to be able to carry on a basic conversation and present a short talk in Cantonese. It took Mr. Benson several years to be able to preach fluently in Cantonese, and Mrs. Benson never mastered the language, as she was tone deaf. The Benson's daughters, who attended school with Chinese students, had Chinese playmates and a Chinese nanny, were fluent in Cantonese at a young age, able to translate simple conversations for their parents.

The written language, consisting of characters, was much the same throughout China, which proved advantageous for the literature work. Mr. Oldham was the first to learn the characters in support of this important work, producing material that could be read by virtually all literate Chinese.

The difficulty in learning the language was later viewed as a mixed blessing, as it forced the missionaries to become observers of the Chinese people and their culture for a time. This time of observation led to a much greater appreciation and understanding of the unique customs and manners of the people, essential to a successful work.

Culture and Gender Traditions

Gender traditions, especially restrictions on women, were a frequent hindrance to the work of the missionaries. Single Chinese women who had been taught by the missionaries were often afraid to embrace Christianity. Both they and their parents feared that if they became Christians, no man would want to marry them. With little opportunity for education, and virtually no chance of advancing economically, having a husband was critical to their very survival. These women could thus not become Christians until they were married and their husbands had first embraced Christianity. Complicating matters, customs in China prohibited a male evangelist from teaching a woman outside of a public meeting. Christian women who were fluent in the language were thus critical to the teaching of the Chinese women.

Paternal control of the family was another cultural hindrance to the acceptance of Christianity. Young men who desired to embrace Christianity could not do so if forbidden by the family patriarch. Regardless of marital status, economic standing, or age of the child, the father's word ruled the household. Young men often had no opportunity to become a Christian while an objecting father was still alive. Complicating matters, Chinese custom did not allow children to become teachers of their parents, regardless of the child's age. It was also difficult for a young evangelist to advise the older men in matters of religion, except in a public or indirect way.[1] This "clannishness" kept many from giving the Christian message serious consideration.[2]

Religious Traditions

While still in Hong Kong, Mrs. Benson often visited Chinese women in their homes. She noted that the women were happy to hear that Jesus came to earth to bring salvation to man, but the idea that they themselves had sins and needed repentance was "not so pleasing to them."[3]

While preaching in the Kochow district of Kwang Tung Province, Mr. Benson discovered that the religious traditions of the Chinese gave them little or no background with which to associate the "strange facts" of the Christian message. Many of the lessons brought ideas very new and very different from anything they had ever heard.[4]

Mr. Oldham wrote that the Chinese people seemed to have no concept of a loving God who was interested in the welfare of the individual man. Based on their religious traditions, such an idea was inconceivable. He also observed that they had very little notion of sin, with their sense of sin largely limited to murder, arson, and treason against the government.[5] Many viewed the Christian church as a sort of society that might be good to belong to in case of death or trouble, but with "no conviction of sin, no idea of repentance, nor any notion of real obedience to God."[6] As a

---

1. George Benson, "Paternal Control in the Orient," 2.
2. Lewis Oldham, "Clannishness," 1.
3. Sallie Benson, letter to supporters, May 1, 1928.
4. George Benson, letter to supporters, May 1, 1928.
5. Lewis Oldham, "Religious Background," January 1931, 3.
6. Lewis Oldham, "Kau Yuk Road Church of Christ," 1.

result, the missionaries believed their most difficult religious hindrance was that of "convincing the Chinese of sin and his need for a redeemer."[7]

If Christianity could meet a real need in life and if it could tolerate the old religions, it might be welcomed. The danger, however, was that the converts would compromise with the older religions by blending their new faith with the old.[8] The exclusive nature of the Christian religion thus caused some converts to either lose their Christian identity or completely abandon their new faith.

Chinese Attitudes toward Foreigners and Missionaries

The anti-foreigner and anti-missionary sentiment in China ebbed and flowed throughout the years of the Canton Mission.

The Boxer Rebellion of 1900 had been an attempt by the Chinese to rid the country of all foreigners. The "Boxers," the Society of the Righteous and Harmonious Fists, believed that China had been severely abused by foreigners, and the missionaries were the most hated of all. The Chinese had heard accusations that missionaries had committed atrocities beyond belief. They also resented the Christian missionaries' assumption that their religion was superior to all Chinese religions. The hostilities continued even after the rebellion was repressed by foreign forces.[9]

After the revolution that overthrew the Qing dynasty (1644–1911), Sun Yat-Sen, the leader of the revolution, was elected president.[10] Sun himself was a Christian, and during his years as president until his death in 1925, Christians were in general treated more decently by the Chinese people. The Communists, however, were militantly anti-religious. Even before Sun's death they organized anti-religious movements, and stirred up other

---

7. Lewis Oldham, "Defects and Errors of Confucianism," 1.
8. Lewis Oldham, "Religious Background," April 1931, 5.
9. Perkins, "Boxer Uprising," 41–42.
10. Perkins, "Sun Yat-Sen," 492–95.

Appendix C

radical political elements to oppose any religious activity. The Christians were portrayed as the imperialists and capitalists from nations that opposed Communism. Following Sun's death, military leader Chiang Kai-Shek became the leader of the Nationalist Party.[11] Conditions on the mainland were very difficult for Christian missionaries until Chiang turned against the Communists, but by 1928 conditions had improved.

The workers of the Canton Mission faced intense anti-missionary sentiment at times, especially in the interior villages. The Chinese there had little outside contact and were very suspicious of foreigners. They did not believe that the missionary was there for their good, but viewed him as a "foreign devil," with evil intentions for the Chinese people. Factions stirred up by the Communists threatened the Bensons in the village of Kwei Hsien in 1926, forcing them to return to the coastal region.[12] In the village of Pong Woo, Mr. Davis was threatened by mob violence so serious that government soldiers were called in to provide protection. The missionaries often had attempts at evangelistic "street preaching" disrupted by noisy, unruly crowds. As Mr. Benson later noted, the missionaries went among a strange people, "uninvited, unannounced, and unwanted."[13]

In the coastal urban areas such as Canton, the Chinese often thought of the missionaries as motivated by the same greed as the unscrupulous commercial agents who preyed on the Chinese people. In their eyes, the missionaries were present only to exploit the people in some way. Any acts of benevolence were seen as part of a scheme to win the people's trust in order to later take advantage of them.[14]

---

11. Perkins, "Chiang Kai-Shek," 69–72.
12. Sallie Benson, *Chats about China*, 100–110.
13. George Benson, "Can We Accomplish More," 1–2.
14. Lewis Oldham, "Some Missionary Problems," October 1931, 5.

Hindrances to the Work
Missionary Misconceptions

One of the early misconceptions of the missionaries was that the Chinese were eager to embrace Christianity. "Missionary propaganda," in the form of enthusiastic sermons and optimistic journal articles, presented an unrealistic picture of the opportunities in the China field. In his last sermon prior to leaving for China in 1925, Mr. Benson spoke of the proposed work in China, and that the Chinese "by the thousands are literally begging to be taught the religion of Christ."[15] The prevalent idea was that the Chinese were standing with outstretched arms longing to receive the missionary and his message. After three years in the Orient, Mr. Oldham commented that the Chinese people were not "angels sitting in the darkness" waiting for an opportunity to hear the Christian message.[16] In fact, the great majority of the Chinese common people were neither anti-Christian, nor pro-Christian, but were indifferent toward the Christian message.[17] They were very proud of and quite satisfied with the ancient religions. For the missionaries, this meant the work would be very slow and very difficult, requiring great patience and skill.

New recruits to China were often greatly disappointed upon their arrival to the foreign field, as everything was much different than expected. The attitude of indifference toward the message was not expected, and the spiritual development of the few converts seemed lacking. The mission fields seemed to be already claimed by other missionary societies, newcomers to the field were viewed as intruders, and the older missionaries were so human. Traveling and living conditions were also much worse than expected.

Preparation for the mission field was difficult for missionaries sent from the Churches of Christ. With no missionary societies available to offer formal training, the missionaries had to rely mainly on personal letters and reports, occasional articles in church publications, and rarely, presentations made by

---

15. Owen, "Five Missionaries Gone," 1.
16. Lewis Oldham, letter to supporters, February 22, 1929.
17. George Benson, "Realities of Missionary Work," January 1930, 6.

Appendix C

missionaries at home on furlough. Classes on mission work were virtually unheard of at this time in the Churches of Christ colleges, although Mr. Benson initiated and taught such a class at Harding College while on furlough in 1932.

Reflecting upon his work in China, Mr. Benson wrote that he had realized in 1925 they were "coming to China blind," but there had been no one in the Churches of Christ to provide the necessary preparation. Training was needed in the future so that new missionaries to the China field could avoid the "several years of rather indefinite blundering" that he had experienced.[18] Upon his return to the states to become president of Harding College, Mr. Benson developed and taught a "Missionary Technique" class which included an overview of the "most effective methods" being applied in the China mission field. The course also included a study of the health problems and living conditions that would be encountered in China.[19]

---

18. George Benson, "Why I Am Returning," 3.
19. Benson, "Missionary Technique," 78–79.

Appendix D

City of Canton in Photographs

THE PHOTOS BELOW ARE intended to give an impression of the day-to-day activities and surroundings of the missionary families living in Canton during the 1920s and 1930s. Many of these photos were taken by the families of the Canton Mission, with additional photos appearing courtesy of Sidney D. Gamble Photographs, David M. Rubenstein Rare Book & Manuscript Library, Duke University.

APPENDIX D

Canton train depot (1930), memorial to Sun Yat-Sen (1935), flower pagoda of an Ancient Buddhist Temple (1935), and typical housing with a Catholic cathedral in the background (1930).

City of Canton in Photographs

Island of Shameen viewed from bridge to Canton mainland, canal through poor neighborhood, ferry boat used to cross the Pearl River, and sampan boat, often used as living quarters for the poor. (These photos courtesy of Sidney D. Gamble Photographs, David M. Rubenstein Rare Book & Manuscript Library, Duke University.)

Appendix D

Canton YMCA, used by the missionary families for recreation and for occasionally holding English or religion classes (1920), Rickshaw puller (1935), Women laborers (1920), Woman laborer with young child (1920). (These photos courtesy of Sidney D. Gamble Photographs, David M. Rubenstein Rare Book & Manuscript Library, Duke University.)

City of Canton in Photographs

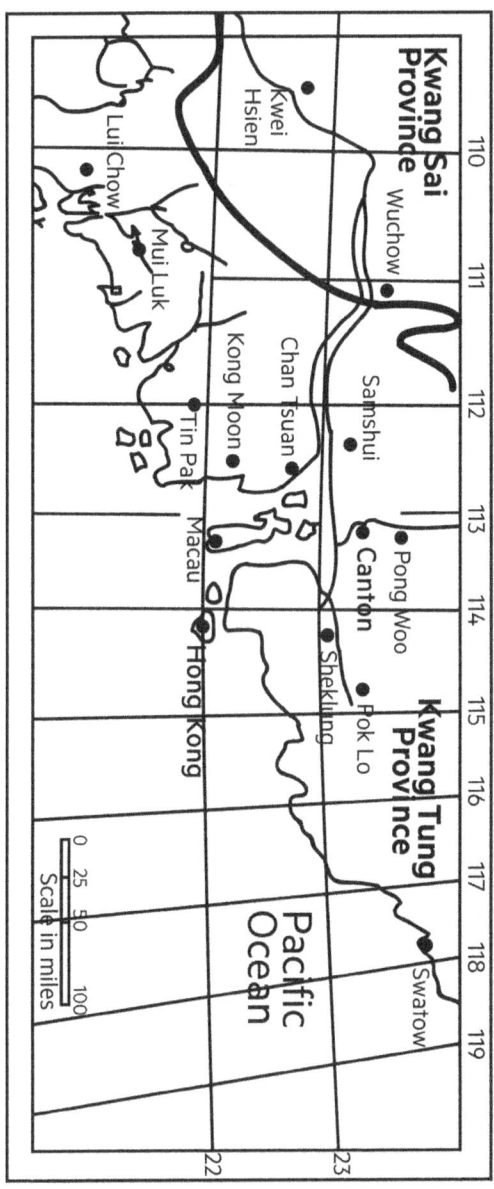

Map of the southern provinces of Kwang Sai and Kwang Tung. Canton was the largest, most prominent city in the southern region of China during the years of the Canton Mission. Its prominence in the region was one of the major factors in choosing Canton as the center for the missionary work. Map produced by Colleen Crowder Templeton.

Bibliography

Bays, Daniel H. "The Growth of Independent Christianity in China, 1900–1937." In *Christianity in China*, 307–16. Stanford: Stanford University Press, 1996.
———. *A New History of Christianity in China.* Chichester, UK: Wiley-Blackwell, 2012.
Benson, George S. "Aim." *Bulletin of the Canton Bible School*, November 1935.
———. "An Announcement." *Oriental Christian*, May 1936.
———. "The Bernards." *Oriental Christian*, June 1936.
———. "The Bible School Building." *Oriental Christian*, November 1934.
———. "Bible School Work." *Oriental Christian*, April 1934.
———. "A Brief Summary." *Oriental Christian*, January 1936.
———. "Can We Accomplish More at Home or Abroad?" *Oriental Christian*, March 1936.
———. "The Canton Bible School." *Oriental Christian*, May 1935.
———. "Canton Bible School Building." *World Vision*, February 1947.
———. "Canton Bible School Building Finished." *Oriental Christian*, December 1934.
———. "The Canton Christian." *Canton Christian*, October 1929.
———. "China Sunday." *Oriental Christian*, January 1934.
———. "Coming to China." *Oriental Christian*, September 1932.
———. "Curriculum." *Bulletin of the Canton Bible School*, November 1935.
———. "Eighty Years Behind." *Canton Christian*, January 1930.
———. "Faculty." *Bulletin of the Canton Bible School*, November 1935.
———. "God's Revelation." *Oriental Christian*, September 1933.
———. "The Honor Roll." *Oriental Christian*, June 1934.
———. "The Honor Roll." *Oriental Christian*, August 1934.
———. "How to Accomplish the Impossible." *Oriental Christian*, November 1934.
———. "The Japanese Invasion." *Oriental Christian*, June 1933.
———. "Leaving Chicago." *Oriental Christian*, December 1931.
———. *Missionary Experiences.* Delight, AR: Gospel Light, 1987.
———. "Missionary Technique." *Harding College Catalog*, 1937–38.

BIBLIOGRAPHY

———. "Name and Object." *Constitution of the Canton Bible School*, 1935.
———. "Paternal Control in the Orient." *Canton Christian*, January 1930.
———. "Payment to Be Made at Once." *Oriental Christian*, April 1936.
———. "A Plan with a Purpose." *Oriental Christian*, June 1933.
———. "Present Activities in Canton." *Oriental Christian*, January 1933.
———. "Present Activities in Canton." *Oriental Christian*, October 1932.
———. "Realities of Missionary Work in China." *Canton Christian*, January 1930.
———. "Realities of Missionary Work in China." *Canton Christian*, January 1931.
———. "Renew Your Subscription Now." *Oriental Christian*, November 1933.
———. "Sister Whitfield." *Oriental Christian*, December 1935.
———. "This and That." *Oriental Christian*, February 1934.
———. "Two Steps by Faith." *Canton Christian*, April 1930.
———. "Why I Am Returning to the States." *Oriental Christian*, June 1936.
Benson, Sallie E. *Chats about China*. Hong Kong: Kae Shean Printing, 1927.
———. "Children's Page." *Oriental Christian*, July 1933.
———. "The Classes." *Oriental Christian*, March 1936.
———. "Gardner-Whitfield Wedding Solemnized." *Oriental Christian*, August 1935.
———. "Personal Glimpses." *Canton Christian*, January 1930.
Bernard, Elizabeth. "Dear Friends." *Oriental Christian*, December 1934.
———. "Travelling Interior." *Oriental Christian*, March 1937.
Brook, Timothy. "Toward Independence: Christianity in China under the Japanese Occupation, 1937-1945." In *Christianity in China*, edited by Daniel H. Bays, 317-37. Stanford: Stanford University Press, 1996.
Davis, Lowell. "Davis Visits Family Here Awaiting Return to China." *Harding Bison*, April 30, 1946.
———. "Evangelistic Meetings." *Oriental Christian*, November 1936.
———. "The Gospel in China." *Harding Bulletin*, June 15, 1946.
———. "Lowell Davis Letter." *Word and Work*, June 1940.
———. "The Open Door in China." *Firm Foundation*, January 6, 1948.
———. "Our Work in China." *Oriental Christian*, March 1937.
———. "Report from China." *Firm Foundation*, July 8, 1947.
Davis, Odessa. *To China and Beyond: A Spiritual Journey*. Austin: Nortex, 2000.
———. "Experiences." *Oriental Christian*, February 1935.
Foster, Douglas A., et al., eds. *The Encyclopedia of the Stone-Campbell Movement*. Grand Rapids: Eerdmans, 2004.
Ho, Virgil. *Understanding Canton*. New York: Oxford University Press, 2005.
Holloway, Gary. "The Current State of Hermeneutics in the Churches of Christ." Paper prepared for the Stone-Campbell Dialogue, June 2006.
Janes, Don Carlos. "Missionary Notes." *Word and Work*, September 1942.
———. "On Foreign Fields." *Word and Work*, December 1922.
Latourette, Kenneth Scott. *A History of Christian Missions in China*. London: Society for Promoting Christian Knowledge, 1929.

Bibliography

Miller, James. *Chinese Religions in Contemporary Societies*. Santa Barbara, CA: ABC-CLIO, 2006.
Morehead, B. D. "Among the Churches." *Oriental Christian*, August 1932.
Oldham, Grace E. "Summer Activities." *Oriental Christian*, August 1937.
———. *Things Chinese*. Keenesburg, CO: Christian Press, 1984.
Oldham, Lewis T. "Back Home Again." *Oriental Christian*, February 1935.
———. "Bible Study Course." *Canton Christian*, April 1930.
———. "Clannishness." *Oriental Christian*, January 1937.
———. "Commentary on Acts in Chinese." *Oriental Christian*, October 1931.
———. "Defects and Errors of Confucianism." *Oriental Christian*, June 1937.
———. "Financial Report." *Canton Christian*, April 1930.
———. "Growth of the Canton Work." *Canton Christian*, January 1931.
———. *Is There Really a God?* Murfreesboro, TN: Dehoff, 1965.
———. "Kau Yuk Road Church of Christ." *Oriental Christian*, December 1936.
———. "Religious Background of the Chinese People." *Canton Christian*, January 1931.
———. "Religious Background of the Chinese People." *Oriental Christian*, April 1931.
———. "Some Missionary Problems." *Oriental Christian*, January 1932.
———. "Some Missionary Problems." *Oriental Christian*, October 1931.
Owen, Felix G. "Five Missionaries Gone." *Apostolic Missions* 1.1 (1925) 1.
Perkins, Dorothy. "Ancestor Worship." In *Encyclopedia of China: The Essential Reference to China, Its History, and Culture*, 11–12. New York: Roundtable, 1999.
———. "Boxer Uprising." In *Encyclopedia of China: The Essential Reference to China, Its History, and Culture*, 41–42. New York: Roundtable, 1999.
———. "Buddhism." In *Encyclopedia of China: The Essential Reference to China, Its History, and Culture*, 47–50. New York: Roundtable, 1999.
———. "Chiang Kai-Shek." In *Encyclopedia of China: The Essential Reference to China, Its History, and Culture*, 69–72. New York: Roundtable, 1999.
———. "Chinese Climate." In *Encyclopedia of China: The Essential Reference to China, Its History, and Culture*, 95. New York: Roundtable, 1999.
———. "Confucianism." In *Encyclopedia of China: The Essential Reference to China, Its History, and Culture*, 100–102. New York: Roundtable, 1999.
———. "Daoism." In *Encyclopedia of China: The Essential Reference to China, Its History, and Culture*, 117–19. New York: Roundtable, 1999.
———. "Guangdong Province." In *Encyclopedia of China: The Essential Reference to China, Its History, and Culture*, 192–93. New York: Roundtable, 1999.
———. "Sun Yat-Sen." In *Encyclopedia of China: The Essential Reference to China, Its History, and Culture*, 492–95. New York: Roundtable, 1999.
Pew Research Center. "Methodology for China." Appendix C of *Global Christianity: A Report on the Size and Distribution of the World's Christian Population*, by the Pew Forum on Religion and Public Life. 2011. http://www.pewforum.org/files/2011/12/ChristianityAppendixC.pdf.
Prout, Elmer. "A California Girl in China." *Pacific Church News*, summer 2002.

BIBLIOGRAPHY

Spence, Jonathan D. *The Search for Modern China*. New York: Norton, 1991.

Tsin, Michael. *Nation, Governance and Modernity in China: Canton, 1900–1927*. Stanford: Stanford University Press, 1999.

Tune, Tom. *Ah Wing's Elizabeth Bernard: Forty Years among the Chinese*. Delight, AR: Gospel Light, 1975.

West, Earl Irvin. *The Search for the Ancient Order*. Vol. 4. Germantown, TN: Religious Book Service, 1987.

Whitfield, Roy. "Doing What We Can." *Oriental Christian*, July 1937.

———. "How We Spend Our Sundays." *Oriental Christian*, July 1933.

———. "New Missionaries for Canton, China." *Oriental Christian*, July 1937.

———. "Vision." *Oriental Christian*, July 1936.

———. "The War Scare in Canton." *Oriental Christian*, August 1937.

———. "Who Wants a Good Position?" *Oriental Christian*, January 1937.

Whitfield, Ruth. "Excerpts from the Bensons' Letters." *Oriental Christian*, September 1936.

———. "A Village Trip." *Oriental Christian*, April 1936.

Williams, D. Newell., et al., eds. *The Stone-Campbell Movement: A Global History*. St. Louis: Chalice, 2013.

Index

Abilene Christian College, xx, 40
ancestor worship, 101, 105
Andrew Jackson, American steamer, 65
Armstrong, John Nelson (J.N.), xvii–xviii, 1–3, 31, 55, 91
Asama Maru, 71

Benson, George, xvi–xxvii, 1–8, 14–25, 28, 31–34, 37–43, 52–56, 60–64, 76–79, 83, 87–92, 100, 106, 108, 110–14
Benson, Lois, 24, 35
Benson, Ruth, xx, 4n3, 5–6, 35
Benson, Sallie Hockaday, xvi–xx, xxvi–xxvii, 2–4, 7, 18, 20, 24, 28, 34–37, 46, 49, 54, 56, 108, 110
Bernard, Elizabeth, xxiii, 39–46, 49–50, 53–61, 65–66, 71–73, 79, 85–92
Bernard, Mrs. Estella, 39–40, 50, 59–60, 86, 90
Boll, R.H., xviii, 39
Boxer Rebellion, 111
Broaddus, Emmett, xx, 5–6, 17, 39, 66
Broaddus, Margaret Neal, xx, 5–6, 39
Buddhism, 101–5, 116
Burke, Corrie Whitten, 64–65
Burke, Leslie, 64–65

Canton (Guangzhou), xxvi, 4, 7–20, 24–28, 34–39, 50–51, 58, 60, 65, 68–76, 86–89, 112, 115–19
Canton Bible School, 29, 32–34, 42–45, 49–58, 63–64, 69–70, 78–82, 88–90, 99–100, 107
Canton Christian, xxvii, 18, 24
Canton English Finishing School, 34, 40, 46, 50, 54–55, 58–59
Canton YMCA, 53, 118
Cantonese language, 15–16, 35, 43, 61, 108–9
Chan Tsuan, 50, 53–54, 58
Chiang, Kai-Shek, 9, 88, 112
Churches of Christ, xv–xxvii, 1–2, 5n6, 18, 40, 76, 95–96, 107, 113–14
Communist Party of China, xvi, 9, 17, 76, 80–90, 111–12
Confucianism, 101–5
Cordell Christian College, xviii, 2
Cornell Avenue Church of Christ (Chicago), 25
Cox, James, 40
Curtis, Earline Franklin, 75, 79–81, 84
Curtis, Frank, 75, 79–87, 92

Davis, Avonelle, xxiii, 71, 73
Davis, Cline, 72, 73

Index

Davis, Lowell, xx, 25, 30–39, 43–44, 49–61, 64, 70–76, 77n4, 78–92, 99–100, 108, 112
Davis, Odessa White, 31, 39, 43–44, 49–50, 54–60, 70–73, 76, 79–80, 85–88, 92
Daxin Department Store, 13
Disciples of Christ, xxv–xxvi

forwarding agent, 1n2, 95–97

Harding College (University), xv, xxvii–xxiii, 2–3, 25, 31, 55, 60–64, 70, 76, 77n4, 79–82, 89–92, 114
Harding, James A., xviii, 2
Harper College, xviii, 1–3
Hong Kong, xxvi, 4–8, 15, 21, 24, 31, 39, 64–71, 76, 86–90, 110

Janes, Don Carlos, xvii–xviii, 1n2, 96
Japanese threat, 16, 31, 55, 71, 73

Kau Yuk Road Church of Christ, 35, 54–59, 69, 99
Kochow, 110
Kunming, 73
Kwang Sai (Guangxi) Province, 4, 6, 15, 17, 89, 108, 119
Kwang Tung (Guangdong) Province, 7, 9, 15, 20, 108, 110, 119
Kwei Hsien, 4–5, 112
Kweilin, 72–73

Lau, P.W., 45, 49, 53, 57, 63, 99
Lei, P.Y., 63
Leung, Hoi Kit, 29–30, 33, 45, 49, 53–57, 60, 63, 66, 69–81, 85–90, 99
Leung, Tit Fei (Ted), 81, 89
Lewis, Jack, 90
Lingnan University, xxvi, 69
living link congregation, 95
Loi So, 39, 60

Macau, 68–72
Man Fuk Lo chapel, 25–28, 106
Mandarin language, 16, 108
Mao, Zedong, xvi, 88
Mattley, Ethel, 5–7, 17, 66, 71
McGarvey's *Commentary on Acts*, 26–27, 62, 76
Mindoro, Philippines, 7
Morehead, B.D., 96
Morrilton, AR, Church of Christ, 2, 28
Mui Luk, 20–21

Nationalist Party of China, 9, 88, 112
Ng Chuen, 28

Oldham, Grace Narron, 3, 18, 29, 33, 49, 54, 57, 59, 63
Oldham, Lewis, xx, xxvii, 1–8, 15–17, 21, 24–29, 33–34, 45, 49, 52–55, 57–63, 65, 70, 92, 98, 99–100, 106, 109–110, 113
Oriental Christian, xxvii, 14, 18, 24–25, 28, 34, 37, 40, 44, 49, 55–61, 64, 96, 98, 106–7

pattern hermeneutics, 107
Pearl Harbor, 67
Pearl River, 9–10, 19, 72, 117
Pepperdine, George, 7
Pinamalayan, Philippines, 7
Pong Woo, 38–39, 43, 49, 112

Qing Dynasty, 9, 13, 111

school for the poor, 44, 50–51, 57
Sham Shui Po Church of Christ, 5, 21
Sincere Company, 13
So, Tin Wong, 17, 21, 25, 28–29, 33, 45, 49, 52–53, 57, 62, 65–66, 70–72, 90, 99
Southern Commercial College (SCC), 77–78, 81–83, 89
Stanley Internment Camp, 71

Index

Stone-Campbell tradition, xxv–xxvi, 1, 5n6, 21, 91, 95
Sun, Yat-Sen, 8, 111, 116
Sun, Yat-Sen University, 19

Taoism, 101–2
threefold strategy, 17, 28, 32, 55
Three-Self Movement, 97
Tung Shan Fan Church of Christ, 19, 26, 31, 106

University of Chicago, 24

Wan, Sheung Yi (Shirley), 81–82, 89
Wan, William, 78, 81
Whitfield, Ruth Gardner, 45–46, 52, 54, 57, 59, 62
Whitfield, Roy, xx, 25, 30–35, 37, 39, 43, 45, 50, 52–53, 55–65, 69–70, 92, 100

www.ingramcontent.com/pod-product-compliance
Lightning Source LLC
Chambersburg PA
CBHW071509150426
43191CB00009B/1457